LIVING WORD! LIVING WATER!

Adventurers

YEAR B

Susan Sayers

with Father Andrew Moore

TWENTY-THIRD PUBLICATIONS
BAYARD Mystic, CT 06355

YEAR B

Adventurers

First published in 1999 in Great Britain by
KEVIN MAYHEW LTD
Buxhall
Stowmarket
Suffolk IP14 3BW

North American copyright © Susan Sayers 2000
Twenty-Third Publications/ Bayard
185 Willow Street
P.O. Box 180
Mystic, CT 06355
(860) 536-2611
(800) 321-0411

ISBN: 1-58595-101-3
Printed in U.S.A.

The other titles in the *Living Word! Living Water! Year B* series are

Complete Resource Book	ISBN 1-58595-098-X
Seekers	ISBN 1-58595-099-8
Explorers	ISBN 1-58595-100-5

Edited by Katherine Laidler
Illustrations by Fred Chevalier

Foreword

While many churches provide for the needs of the children, there is often an uncomfortable gap where young people are concerned. This is the age when deep questions are being asked, and it is essential that our young people find in their churches those who are going to listen and not be shocked; those who are willing to enter into real discussion and provide relevant and unsuffocating support during adolescence.

Many churches are well aware of the needs, but find it difficult to provide for them. They are concerned about this age group feeling too old for children's liturgy but not able to relate to what adults are doing in church. Sadly, the result is often an exodus of young people, just when their faith could be (and often is) taking off.

Not only do our young people need the Church; the Church badly needs its young people. Their insistence on rejecting every hint of hypocrisy, and their gift of presenting challenging ideas with wit and enthusiasm—these are good for everyone and vital for a healthy body of Christ.

This program aims to provide relevant and varied activities for young people which stimulate their thinking and encourage valuable discussion. Although some young people may be involved on the children's liturgy team, I am convinced that they need feeding at their own level as well.

The factfiles on each week's activity sheet can be collected into a book so that the course becomes a reference manual. It could also be used as an ongoing course for Confirmation.

All the material in the book is copyright-free for non-commercial use.

SUSAN SAYERS
with Father Andrew Moore

This book is dedicated to my family and friends,
whose encouraging support has been wonderful,
and to all those whose good ideas are included here for others to share.

Acknowledgments

The publishers wish to express their gratitude to the following for permission to reproduce their copyright material in this publication:

The Copyright Company, Nashville, TN, for *Jesus is Lord!* (verse 1), © 1980, Word's Spirit of Praise, administered by Maranatha! Music c/o The Copyright Co. All rights reserved. International copyright secured. Used by permission.

Darton, Longman & Todd Ltd, 1 Spencer Court, 140-142 Wandsworth High Street, London, SW18 4JJ, UK, for the extract from *Audacity to Believe* by Sheila Cassidy, © 1992 Darton, Longman & Todd Ltd.

EMI Christian Music Publishing, P.O. Box 5085, Brentwood, TN 37024, for *Be Still, For the Presence of the Lord* (verse 3), © 1986 Kingsway's Thankyou Music; *I'm Accepted, I'm Forgiven*, © 1985 Kingsway's Thankyou Music; *Meekness and Majesty* (verse 2 and chorus), © 1986 Kingsway's Thankyou Music; and *The King is Among Us* (verse 1), © 1981 Kingsway's Thankyou Music; and *Spirit of the Living God*, © 1935, 1963 Birdwing Music. All rights in the Western Hemisphere administered by EMI Christian Music Publishing.

GIA Publications Inc., 7404 S. Mason Avenue, Chicago, IL 60638, for *Jesus Christ is Waiting* (verse 2). Taken from *Enemy of Apathy* (1988 Wild Goose Publications).

Hodder & Stoughton Ltd, 338 Euston Road, London, NW1 3BH, UK, for the extract from *Child of the Covenant* by Michelle Guinness. Used by permission.

Hope Publishing Co., Carol Stream, IL 60188, for *Lord For the Years* (verse 5).

Make Way Music, P.O. Box 263, Croydon, CR9 5AP, UK, for *Shine, Jesus, Shine* (chorus). All rights reserved. International copyright secured. Used by permission.

Mercy/Vineyard Publishing, PO Box 68025, Anaheim, CA 92817, for *Purify My Heart* (chorus), © 1990.

OCP Publications, 5536 NE Hassalo, Portland, OR 97213, for *Make Me a Channel of Your Peace* (dedicated to Mrs. Francis Tracy) and *All That I Am* by Sebastian Temple (1967 OCP Publications). All rights reserved. Used by permission.

Paulist Press, 997 Macarthur Blvd., Mahwah, NJ 07430, for the extract from *A Glimpse of Glory* by Gonville ffrench-Beytagh.

Josef Weinberger Ltd, 12-14 Mortimer Street, London, W1N 7RD, UK, for *Lord Jesus Christ* (last verse) and *O Lord, All the World* (verse 4). Used by permission.

Contents

Teaching programs and activity sheets for the following Special Feasts will be found in the *Adventurers* book for Year A.

Mary, Mother of God—January 1

The Presentation of the Lord (Candlemas)—February 2

Saint John the Baptist—June 24

Saints Peter and Paul—June 29

The Transfiguration of the Lord—August 6

The Assumption—August 15

The Triumph of the Holy Cross—September 14

All Saints—November 1

Feasts of the Dedication of a Church

Christmas Day

Christmas Day is very much a time for all God's children to worship together, and I have not included separate ideas or activity sheets for the young people.

Use some of the All-age suggestions in the *Living Word! Living Water! Complete Resource Book,* or involve the young people in planning part of the service, and in the music group or choir, as servers, welcomers, collectors of the offering, decorating the church and so on.

Advent

First Sunday of Advent

Thought for the day
Be alert and watchful; keep yourselves ready.

Readings
Isaiah 63:16–17, 64:1, 3–8
1 Corinthians 1:3–9
Mark 13:33–37

Aim: To sense the longing for the Messiah and the need for rescue.

Starter
Try this short sketch about "waiting" on page 125.

Teaching
Start by reading the passage from Isaiah, drawing out the way it moves in mood from "If only" through "But heck!" to "Still, maybe?" Then look at 1 Corinthians 1. What has happened in the meantime to account for the hope and confidence expressed in Paul's letter? It is the life, death and resurrection of Jesus the Christ that has turned everything around.

Remind them that not only did Jesus come as our Savior two thousand years ago, he is also going to come again, but this time in the full glory of God. Read the gospel from Mark 13 and pick up on the clues and the unknowns, and the need to be watchful and ready.

Praying
O Lord, you are our Father.
We are the clay, you are the potter;
we are all the work of your hand.
Oh look upon us as we pray,
for we are all your people
in need of your mercy.

Activities
On the activity sheet there are prophets waiting in line at a bus stop with Bible references in their speech bubbles, so that the growing sense of need and longing for rescue is explored. There is also a selection of disaster pictures that link with the human condition spiritually and our need for rescue.

Discussion starters
1. Why does Jesus advise us to be alert and watchful?
2. How does the expectation of Jesus coming again with great power and glory affect the way we think and speak and act and spend in the meantime?

Notes

10

Second Sunday of Advent

Thought for the day

John the Baptist prepares the way for the coming of the Messiah by helping the people to realign their lives.

Readings

Isaiah 40:1–5, 9–11
2 Peter 3:8–14
Mark 1:1–8

Aim: To look at Mark's treatment of John the Baptist's ministry, and the fulfillment of Isaiah's prophecy.

Starter

Have one of those frog toys with a suction pad that you press down and wait until it suddenly hops. (Or a rubber thimble for separating sheets of paper works just as well.) Have the children take turns setting up the toy. Have them all shout, "Now!" when they think it will pop up or hop.

Teaching

Read the beginning of Mark's gospel, noticing how we are suddenly in the center of all the action, and John seems to appear as if from nowhere. (Compare this with the first reference we get to the prophet Elijah's sudden appearance in 1 Kings 17:1.) Mark starts his account of Jesus with his public ministry, rather than the birth events, and John the Baptist is clearly the "Elijah," the voice in the desert, which the prophets had foretold.

Have a look at that prophecy in Isaiah 40, and look at how John was fulfilling it. See how the prophet is foretelling both the coming of Jesus in his ministry on earth and his second coming in all God's glory at the end of time.

Go back to the gospel reading and discuss whether John seems to be calling individuals to repentance or the nation as a whole (or both). Why would baptism with water be a helpful symbol of what the people were doing spiritually?

Praying

Show us your unfailing love, O Lord,
and grant us your salvation.
I will listen to what God the Lord will say:
he promises peace to his people, his saints—
but let them not return to folly.
Surely his salvation is near those who fear him,
that his glory may dwell in our land.
(From Psalm 85)

Activities

There are various "watery" experiences on the activity activity sheet to help pick up on the symbolism of water. Children are encouraged to look at different areas of their life which may need sorting out or cleaning up.

Discussion starters

1. Why is a repentant people more likely to be able to receive Jesus the Christ?

2. Forget, for a moment, the traditions of our church, and imagine yourself on the shore of the River Jordan, having been totally immersed in cold water. In the light of this experience, how would you imagine being "baptized with the Holy Spirit"? How did (and does) Jesus do this?

Notes

BAPTISM

WHY DID JOHN DIP PEOPLE UNDER THE WATER?

It's like a code. Water shows cleaning and new life and that stands for the spiritual cleaning and new life.

WAS IT FOR INDIVIDUALS OR THE NATION AS A WHOLE?

Both. Individuals were making a point of cleaning up their lives, and lots of individuals represented the whole of the people of Israel wanting to be clean and ready for God.

Water can...

BAPTISM USES WATER TO BE A SYMBOL OF WHAT IS GOING ON SPIRITUALLY

WHERE DOES OUR NATION NEED TO REPENT AND BE MADE CLEAN?

HABITS?

THE WAY YOU TREAT PEOPLE YOU LIKE?

WHAT NEEDS CLEANSING OR SORTING OUT IN YOUR LIFE?

THINGS YOU CHOOSE TO IGNORE?

WHERE YOU WANT YOUR OWN WAY?

THE WAY YOU TREAT PEOPLE YOU DON'T LIKE?

SHOW US YOUR UNFAILING LOVE, O LORD, AND GRANT US YOUR SALVATION. I WILL LISTEN TO WHAT GOD THE LORD WILL SAY; HE PROMISES PEACE TO HIS PEOPLE, HIS SAINTS ~ BUT LET THEM NOT RETURN TO FOLLY. SURELY HIS SALVATION IS NEAR THOSE WHO FEAR HIM, THAT HIS GLORY MAY DWELL IN OUR LAND.

(—FROM PSALM 84—)

Third Sunday of Advent

Thought for the day
In Jesus, God will be fulfilling the Messianic prophecies about the promised Savior.

Readings
Isaiah 61:1–2, 10–11
1 Thessalonians 5:16–24
John 1:6–8, 19–28

Aim: To see how the coming of the Messiah was God visiting and redeeming his people.

Starter
Each person in turn adds a word to a gradually developing sentence, so that some kind of story, which no one person has planned, starts to take shape.

Teaching
All through the history of the people of Israel words were spoken by the prophets to reveal a bit more about what God meant and what God was like. Gradually the people started to grasp that one day God would be among his people to save them, in a new and very personal way. They started to think in terms of a Messiah, one anointed by God, who would come to them.

Look at the reading from Isaiah 61 to discover what the Messiah would be like. Pick out the characteristics in discussion and make a note of them. Then look at today's gospel, stopping at verse 22, where they ask, "Who are you?" Why might they have thought that John was the Messiah or Elijah? (You can refer to the notes made.) Then read on to find out how John describes himself. Link this with the passage from Isaiah which you've just read. Why did John talk about the Messiah being already among them, though not yet known? (Think back to when John and Jesus had been born.)

Read through the Magnificat, which takes the place of the Psalm today, to see Mary praising God for what an amazing thing he has done. How does her excitement fit in with the Messiah promises, and the people's hopes?

Praying
With all my heart I praise the Lord
and I am glad because of God my Savior.
He helps his servant Israel
and is always merciful to his people.
The Lord made this promise to our ancestors;
to Abraham and his family forever.

(From the Magnificat)

Activities
On the activity sheet there is space to record some of the prophecies foretold about the Messiah, together with other references to look up, which fill out the picture of a promised Savior, given to the people of Israel throughout their history. They are also encouraged to look at what signs we should be expecting to see in a Christian church claiming to be followers of the way of the Messiah (or Christ).

Discussion starters
1. Why did the authorities want to check out John's identity and authority?

2. Examine the advice of the Thessalonians passage and look at how our lives, individually and as the church, measure up.

Notes

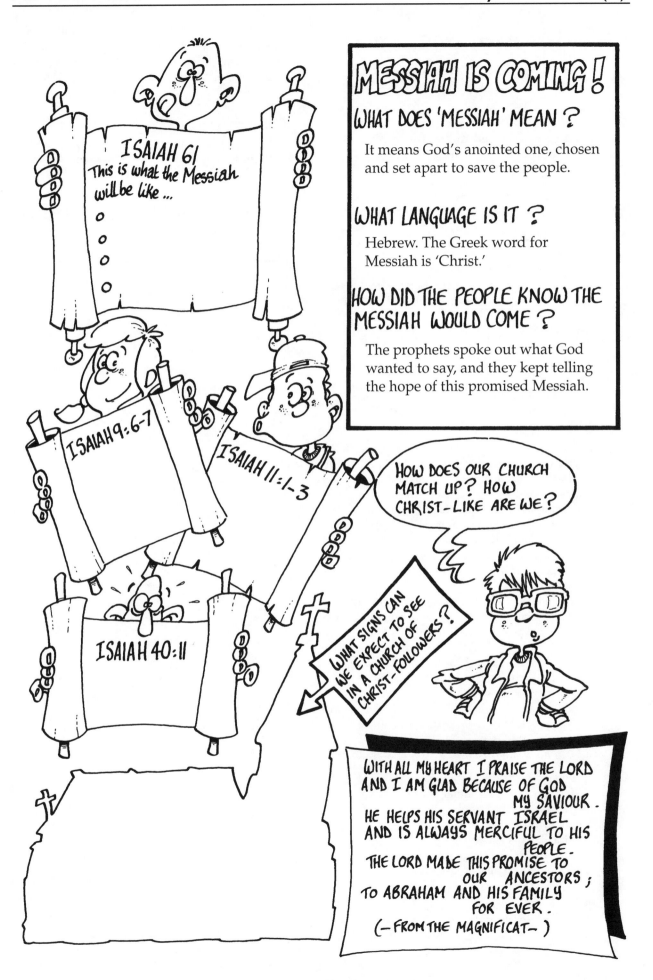

Fourth Sunday of Advent

Thought for the day

God's promised kingdom, announced both to King David in ancient times and to Mary by the angel Gabriel, will go on forever.

Readings

2 Samuel 7, 1–5, 8–12, 14, 16
Romans 16:25–27
Luke 1:26–38

Aim: To see how the hope of a Messiah took shape through the years and was fulfilled in the birth of Jesus.

Starter

Provide crayons to try some "rubbing" on any effective surfaces (for example, coins, relief maps, shoe soles or manhole covers).

Teaching

Today we are looking at a gradually revealed picture of God's plan to save the world. Begin by reading the passage from 2 Samuel 7, noting the details of God's promise about the coming kingdom on a sheet of paper. Explain how, when the monarchy of Israel had crumbled, people started to think of this promised Savior as a spiritual leader, rather than an ordinary worldly king. He became known as God's anointed, or chosen, One—the Messiah.

Then go on to read today's gospel, with different people reading the parts of Mary and Gabriel. Go through the points noted already and tick those that match up. What about the coming king being of the house of David? (See verse 27.) Recap on King David's background (2 Samuel 7:8) and link his position with Mary's in Luke 1:46–55. Draw them to see how the ancient promise is being worked out through good people who make themselves available to God.

Praying

O come, O come, Emmanuel,
and ransom captive Israel,
that mourns in lonely exile here,
until the Son of God appears.
Rejoice, rejoice!
Emmanuel shall come to thee, O Israel.

Activities

On the activity sheet they can explore the nature of the Messiah, both as a priestly and a kingly figure, and there is the script of a conversation between two rocks on a hill near Bethlehem, remembering events there through the years and drawing attention to the historical and spiritual links of today's teaching.

Discussion starters

1. In the light of today's readings, why do you think Jesus put in so much teaching about the nature of the kingdom of God during his earthly ministry?

2. How can we further the kingdom and hasten its full coming?

Notes

DRAMA

ONE BOULDER to ANOTHER BOULDER

1st Rock   Gets cold when the sun's off your back, doesn't it?

2nd Rock   Yeah – look, the lights are being lit down there in Bethlehem already.

1st Rock   Do you remember that shepherd boy who used to sit on me and play his harp in the evenings?

2nd Rock   How could I forget! King David, they made him in the end. What a fine young man he was!

1st Rock   You know what I heard?

2nd Rock   No – what?

1st Rock   There's going to be another shepherd king born soon in Bethlehem – a descendant of our shepherd king, David.

2nd Rock   A son of David! Isn't that the one who's supposed to reign over the whole world for ever?

1st Rock   That's what they've been saying for the last thousand years.

2nd Rock   I wonder if he'll come up here and sit on us?

1st Rock   Mmm, that's a thought. Who knows – if we stick around here for another couple of thousand years...

2nd Rock   ... which we will ...

1st Rock   ... we might become famous, telling our story to other fine young men ...

2nd Rock   ... and women ...

      1st Rock   ... all over the world!

      Both   What a thought!

ONE DAY A SON OF DAVID WILL REIGN

WHY WERE THE PEOPLE SO KEEN ON THEIR GREAT MESSIAH BEING FROM KING DAVID'S FAMILY?

Well, they looked back to David, the shepherd king, as the best king ever – a close friend of God, a good leader, and in touch with ordinary people.

SO THEY HOPED THE MESSIAH WOULD BE AS GOOD?

Better! They hoped God's chosen one would be like a perfect, priestly King David, who would reign for ever.

THAT SOUNDS LIKE JESUS, TO ME?

Yes, God's promise to David was repeated to Mary as she conceived Jesus!

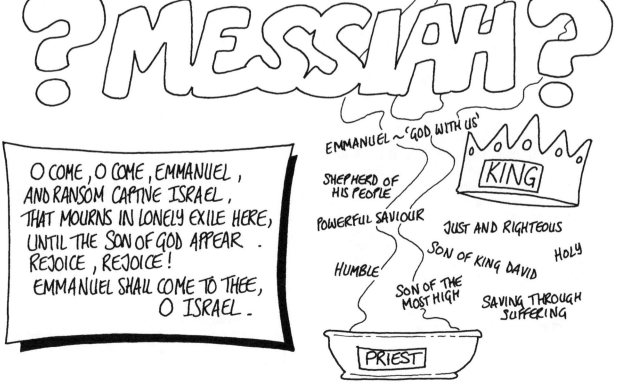

? MESSIAH ?

O COME, O COME, EMMANUEL, AND RANSOM CAPTIVE ISRAEL, THAT MOURNS IN LONELY EXILE HERE, UNTIL THE SON OF GOD APPEAR. REJOICE, REJOICE! EMMANUEL SHALL COME TO THEE, O ISRAEL.

EMMANUEL ~ 'GOD WITH US'

SHEPHERD OF HIS PEOPLE

POWERFUL SAVIOUR

HUMBLE

SON OF THE MOST HIGH

KING

JUST AND RIGHTEOUS

SON OF KING DAVID

HOLY

SAVING THROUGH SUFFERING

PRIEST

First Sunday
of Christmas:
The Holy Family

Thought for the day

The Savior of the world is born as a fully human baby into a real human family.

Readings

Sirach 3:2–6, 12–14
Colossians 3:12–21
Luke 2:22–40

Aim: To look at the Holy Family and learn from it.

Starter

Wedding photos. Give everyone a slip of paper providing them with an identity at a family wedding—bride, bridegroom, bride's mother, best man, chief bridesmaid, ring bearer, and so on. One slip is labeled "official photographer," and this person has to be in charge, calling out for a list of wedding shots, with the appropriate people coming in role to pose for the group photos.

Teaching

Read the passage from Colossians, looking out for the benefits of this kind of attitude and behavior in family life. Talk over the tensions and conflicts of family life which are caused by us living without this clothing of compassion, kindness and humility, gentleness and patience, forbearance and forgiveness. Then take a look at the words from Sirach, which, though written so long ago, ring true with us just as much today. Talk over our treatment of elderly members of our families, their needs and their wealth of time and experience.

The Holy Family had enormous pressures and hardships to face together, and the responsibility of raising God's Son, so it must not have been without its difficulties. Look back over the Colossians reading to see what would have helped and strengthened Mary, Joseph and Jesus during the years of Jesus' upbringing.

Read the gospel for today, noticing the support they also relied on from the faith community, and talk about how our church community supports families, and any ways they feel it could develop such support.

Praying

Lord of all kindliness, Lord of all grace,
your hands swift to welcome,
your arms to embrace;

be there at our homing and give us, we pray,
your love in our hearts, Lord,
at the eve of the day.

Activities

On the activity sheet they can fill in the factfiles of Mary and Joseph and their domestic circumstances, so they see that this was not a family who had it all easy, but a family who prayed together, united in their love of God. There is also a jelly person chart to help them think over where they feel the different members of their family are in relation to one another.

Discussion starters

1. What do you value most about being a member of a family or a member of the church family?

2. What can we learn about Christian parenting, both in the nuclear family and in our church community, from looking at the Holy Family?

Notes

JESUS' FAMILY

WHY DIDN'T GOD PUT JESUS WITH RICH PARENTS WHO COULD GIVE HIM THE BEST OF EVERYTHING?

Perhaps our idea of 'best' is different from God's idea.

HOW DO YOU MEAN?

Well, Jesus had lots of love and protection, and he wasn't cut off from the other children of the town. Both Joseph and Mary were open to God and people of prayer, too.

I SEE WHAT YOU MEAN. ALL THAT IS A DIFFERENT KIND OF 'RICH', ISN'T IT?

Yes – money isn't everything.

IF THIS IS FAMILY LIFE, WHERE ARE YOU? WHERE ARE THE REST OF YOUR FAMILY?

NAME: **MARY**

KNOWN FAMILY:

STATUS:

OCCUPATION:

VOCATION:

DISTANCE TRAVELLED WHILE HEAVILY PREGNANT:

DISTANCE TRAVELLED WITH CHILD UNDER TWO YEARS OLD:

NAME: **JOSEPH**

FAMILY: DESCENDED FROM _____

STATUS:

OCCUPATION:

REASON FOR JOURNEY TO EGYPT:

HARDEST DECISION:

LORD OF ALL KINDLINESS,
LORD OF ALL GRACE,
YOUR HANDS SWIFT TO WELCOME,
YOUR ARMS TO EMBRACE;
BE THERE AT OUR HOMING
AND GIVE US, WE PRAY,
YOUR LOVE IN OUR HEARTS, LORD,
AT THE EVE OF THE DAY.

Second Sunday of Christmas

Thought for the day

The Word made flesh at Christmas was always with God, always expressing his creative love.

Readings

Sirach 24:1–2, 8–12
Ephesians 1:3–6, 15–18
John 1:1–18

Aim: To see how the Word can be seen present from the beginning.

Starter

Play a wordsearch game, where the words are there already and the children just need to find them.

Teaching

First read the gospel for today, noticing the capital W in Word and discussing who John is talking about. In what way is Jesus God's Word? Was God's Word there at the beginning, as John says? (Look at Genesis to check.)

Now look at the Old Testament reading, picking up on the Word (sometimes thought of as the wisdom of God) being there all the time and not suddenly arriving on the hay in Bethlehem from nowhere. (Look at the picture on the sheet.)

Explain how John was writing for the Greek philosophers who would find it helpful to think of God in this way. Link it, too, with what God called himself when talking to Moses (Exodus 3:13–15) and with Jesus' "I AM" teaching (John 8:58, for example).

Praying

Jesus, living Word of God,
you show us what loving means
and what it costs.

Activities

On the activity sheet they are encouraged to see God's Word in terms of the Trinity, and to explore the beginning of John's gospel more deeply, expressing their ideas in drawing.

Discussion starters

1. Why do you think the eternal Word came into our world as a human baby, born as vulnerable and dependent as the rest of us?

2. How does our faith in Jesus affect the way we look at the books of the Old Testament?

Notes

THE WORD — GOD'S WORD

WHY DOES JOHN CALL JESUS THE WORD?

Well, what is someone's word?

I SUPPOSE IT EXPRESSES YOUR THOUGHTS.

Yes, that's right. And Jesus is the expression of God – he expresses God's love to us.

DID THAT START AT BETHLEHEM?

No. God spoke creation into being right at the beginning.

SO IN A WAY THE WORD OF GOD HAD ALWAYS BEEN THERE?

Yes.

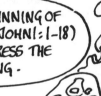

TAKE THE BEGINNING OF JOHN'S GOSPEL (JOHN 1:1-18) AND TRY TO EXPRESS THE IDEA IN DRAWING.

ALWAYS THERE ⇨ GENESIS 1:1-3

BORN ⇨ PSALM 147:15-19

LIFE STORY ⇨ JOHN 1:1-4

JESUS, LIVING WORD OF GOD, YOU SHOW US WHAT LOVING MEANS AND WHAT IT COSTS.

The Epiphany of the Lord

Thought for the day
Jesus, the promised Messiah, is shown to the Gentile world.

Readings
Isaiah 60:1–6
Ephesians 3:2–3a, 5–6
Matthew 2:1–12

Aim: To look at how people "journey" to faith.

Starter
In a circle, pass a bus or train ticket around, and each person in turn says how they got here today. Then pass a cross around. Each person says how they're a Christian, or where they feel they are, how they got here and who has helped them on the way. (As with all circle time, those who don't wish to speak can pass the cross on, and it's fine to say the same as someone else has said if their situation is the same.)

Teaching
Start with today's gospel reading, establishing what we know from the account about where they came from, how many and who they were. Draw attention to their not being Jewish, but pagan foreigners. Imagine together some of the dangers they may have faced on their journey. Why were they wanting to bother with it? How was the king they found different from what they were expecting?

Now look at Ephesians 3 to see how Paul's calling was carrying on the mission to spread the good news to all the non-Jewish people, including us, if we are Gentiles. Finally look at Isaiah 60 to see how this had been prophesied generations before.

Praying
O Lord, our King,
let your kingdom come
in every nation
and every person,
starting with me.
Amen.

Activities
Make a banner or poster that expresses our many different journeys to Christ, who welcomes us wherever we have come from. On the activity sheet there are some examples of such journeys, and space to think about their own journey.

Discussion starters
1. Why do you think Matthew, writing for the Hebrew people, considered this event of the wise men's visit so important to include?
2. What can we, both as Gentiles and as members of the established church, learn from the Magi visit about our own attitudes and calling?

Notes

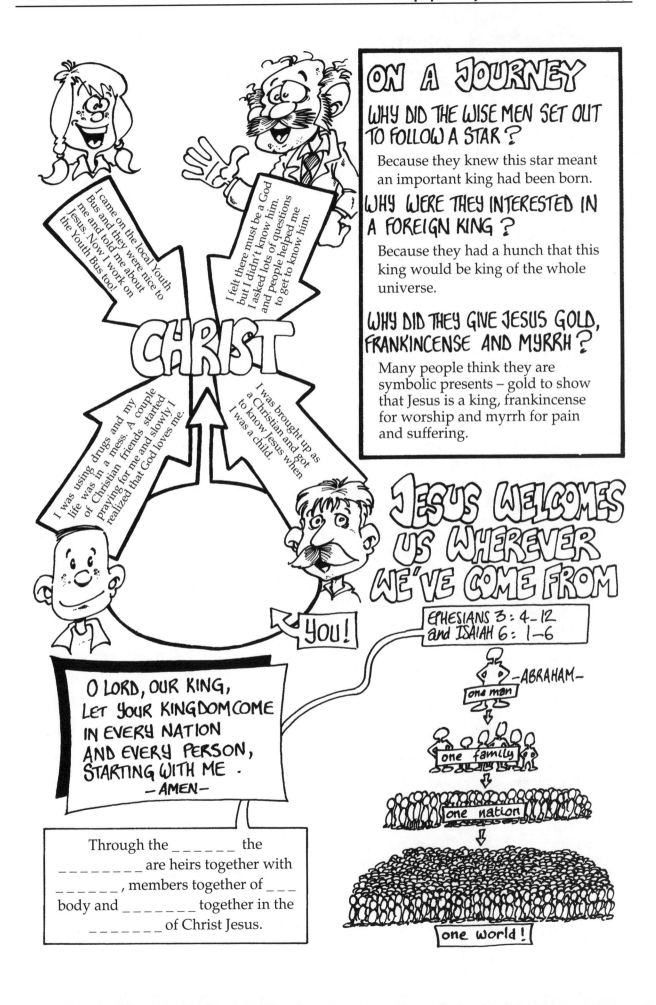

ON A JOURNEY

WHY DID THE WISE MEN SET OUT TO FOLLOW A STAR?

Because they knew this star meant an important king had been born.

WHY WERE THEY INTERESTED IN A FOREIGN KING?

Because they had a hunch that this king would be king of the whole universe.

WHY DID THEY GIVE JESUS GOLD, FRANKINCENSE AND MYRRH?

Many people think they are symbolic presents – gold to show that Jesus is a king, frankincense for worship and myrrh for pain and suffering.

I came on the local Youth Bus and they were nice to me and told me about Jesus. Now I work on the Youth Bus too!

I felt there must be a God but I didn't know him. I asked lots of questions and people helped me to get to know him.

I was using drugs and my life was in a mess. A couple of Christian friends started praying for me and slowly I realized that God loves me.

I was brought up as a Christian and got to know Jesus when I was a child.

CHRIST

YOU!

JESUS WELCOMES US WHEREVER WE'VE COME FROM

EPHESIANS 3: 4-12 and ISAIAH 6: 1-6

—ABRAHAM—
one man

one family

one nation

one world!

O LORD, OUR KING,
LET YOUR KINGDOM COME
IN EVERY NATION
AND EVERY PERSON,
STARTING WITH ME.
— AMEN —

Through the _ _ _ _ _ _ the _ _ _ _ _ _ _ _ are heirs together with _ _ _ _ _ _ _ , members together of _ _ _ body and _ _ _ _ _ _ _ together in the _ _ _ _ _ _ _ of Christ Jesus.

The Baptism of the Lord

Thought for the day

Through the Holy Spirit, Jesus is affirmed at his Baptism as God's beloved Son, and we too are given the Spirit of God, which affirms us as God's adopted daughters and sons.

Readings

Isaiah 42:1–4, 6–7
Acts 10:34–38
Mark 1:7–11

Aim: To explore the presence of the Holy Spirit, particularly at Baptism.

Starter

Play some gentle music and give out paper and paints for them to express in color and form what they hear as the passage from Isaiah is read.

Teaching

Where is the Spirit of God in this passage? Point out the effects it has on the servant and how this looks forward to Jesus.

Now read Mark's account of Jesus' Baptism, noticing how the Spirit of God is portrayed here, and exploring why it might have seemed like a dove. Link this with the words God speaks to affirm Jesus in his identity and his mission.

What are the effects of the Holy Spirit in their own lives? When they sense God's presence, is it like this or different again? Help them to see that God's Spirit comes to fill us only when we genuinely seek God and long to be filled with his life. How the Spirit comes varies, but always there is a sense of inner peace and joy, a deepening of love for God and a deepening realization that God is real, alive and active.

Praying

Spirit of the living God, fall afresh on me!
Spirit of the living God, fall afresh on me!
Melt me, mold me, fill me, use me,
Spirit of the living God, fall afresh on me!
(Daniel Iverson
© 1963 Birdwing Music/EMI Christian Music Publishing)

Activities

The activities on the sheet help them to see how gentle, dynamic and creative the Holy Spirit is revealed to be in creation, in Baptism and in us.

Discussion starters

1. Why do you think Jesus was baptized by John when he didn't need to repent?

2. Is the thought of God's Spirit dwelling in us a little frightening; would we prefer God to keep his distance?

Notes

SPIRIT OF THE LIVING GOD,
FALL AFRESH ON ME !
MELT ME, MOULD ME, FILL ME, USE ME,
SPIRIT OF THE LIVING GOD,
FALL AFRESH ON ME !

(Daniel Iverson
© 1963 Birdwing Music/EMI Christian Music Publishing)

WITH WATER; WITH THE HOLY SPIRIT

WHY DID JOHN BAPTISE PEOPLE?

He washed them in water as a sign that they were being washed clean from their sins.

HOW CAN YOU BE BAPTISED WITH THE HOLY SPIRIT?

This is being soaked and immersed in the living God – quite an experience.

DO YOU MEAN THAT GOD CAN ACTUALLY ENTER OUR LIVING ON A DAY-TO-DAY BASIS?

Yes! You only have to want God to fill your life.

THE HOLY SPIRIT AT CREATION...

THE HOLY SPIRIT IN OUR LIVES...

THE HOLY SPIRIT AT JESUS' BAPTISM...

THE HOLY SPIRIT AT PENTECOST...

THE HOLY SPIRIT OF GOD

GENTLE · ENCOURAGING · REVITALISING · DISTURBING · REAL · ALIVE · REFRESHING · DYNAMIC · CHALLENGING · INVIGORATING · CALMING · ACTIVE · CREATIVE · PEACEFUL · POWERFUL · STRENGTHENING

Lent

First Sunday of Lent

Thought for the day

After his Baptism Jesus is led by the Spirit into the wilderness before returning to proclaim God's kingdom.

Readings

Genesis 9:8–15
1 Peter 3:18–22
Mark 1:12–15

Aim: To look at the value of Jesus' time in the desert and our season of Lent.

Starter

Set up a short orienteering course, with something to collect from each point as they reach it. You will need to make a chart of the area on squared paper, marking the squares with numbers and letters (as shown below) so that they can find their way by map coordinates.

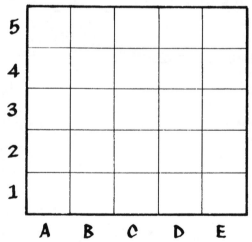

Teaching

Going through life is rather like finding our way through a landscape, and we need maps and a compass to guide us. Jesus referred to himself as the Way, which we can follow and trust. But, before he was able to start on that ministry, he had some working out to do himself.

Read the gospel for today. What happened right after Jesus had been baptized? Did he start his work immediately? No, he went out into the loneliness and discipline of the desert for forty days to search out what his role was, and how he needed to be spending the rest of his life on earth. It was a time of severe and difficult testing, which he had to go through, keeping to the right direction by keeping close to God and his word in Scripture, as the doubts and temptations battled in him.

Only then could he come back into circulation and start his life's work. What are we told his work was? Proclaiming that God's kingdom is very near.

Now look at Noah and his family, setting out into the new, post-flood world. What do they receive from God to set them up for the rebuilding work ahead? God's promise of faithful, sustaining love, in the sign of the rainbow.

Lent gives us a chance to spend the same amount of time as Jesus spent in the desert, facing ourselves and our commitment to living God's way; to live more simply and rigorously while we allow God to prepare us for our own ministry as baptized Christians, proclaiming the risen Christ. It's all carefully thought out that Easter, the festival celebrating Christ's Resurrection, follows straight on from this "desert season" of Lent.

Praying

Lead us, heavenly Father, lead us
o'er the world's tempestuous sea;
guard us, guide us, keep us, feed us,
for we have no help but thee;
yet possessing every blessing
if our God our Father be.

Activities

On the activity sheet there are some desert questions to reflect on, and some more teaching about Lent, with suggestions for using it profitably. Encourage the young people to take part in the parish Lent course, or provide one specifically for them.

Discussion starters

1. Why can God only work with us in earnest when we are totally honest with him?

2. What is it that makes us decide whether or not discipleship is too costly?

Notes

TIME OUT, DESERT STYLE

NOT MUCH TO DO IN A DESERT, IS THERE?

Not a lot. But there's plenty to be.

HOW DO YOU MEAN?

When we haven't got lots of distractions we're forced to face what we're really like.

I'M NOT SURE I WANT TO.

No one's that keen! But it's only when we make the effort to get in touch with our real selves in God's company that he can really start working in our lives.

DESERT QUESTIONS

WHO AM I?

WHICH PARTS OF ME STILL SHUT GOD OUT?

HOW WILL THE WORLD BE BETTER BECAUSE I HAVE LIVED?

HOW HAS GOD BROUGHT ME TO THIS MOMENT?

IS GOD CALLING ME FOR A PARTICULAR KIND OF WORK?

LENT

IS A USEFUL DESERT !!!

IDEAS FOR USING IT...

LEAD US, HEAVENLY FATHER, LEAD US, O'ER THE WORLD'S TEMPESTUOUS SEA; GUARD US, GUIDE US, KEEP US, FEED US, FOR WE HAVE NO HELP BUT THEE; YET POSSESSING EVERY BLESSING IF OUR GOD OUR FATHER BE.

WHAT DO YOU KNOW ABOUT LENT?

Read through the whole of Mark's gospel (that's less than 3 chapters a week).

If your church has a Lent course, join in. (If it hasn't, ask for one!)

Live your life a bit more simply – spend less, for instance.

Write in a DAILY prayer time on your schedule and stick to it.

1. The church color for Lent is

green	
purple	
red	

2. Jesus was in the desert for

		days
42		
7		
40		

3. Christians use Lent to prepare themselves for the festival of

Easter	
Christmas	
Pentecost	

4. Lent is a time for fasting and prayer. Fasting means

practicing self-control by going without food	
practicing for a race by going fast	
practicing prayer by speaking quickly	

Second Sunday of Lent

Thought for the day

Christ's willingness to face suffering and death, in order to save us, proclaims the total sacrificial love of God.

Readings

Genesis 22:1–2, 9–13, 15–18
Romans 8:31–34
Mark 9:2–10

Aim: To see that Jesus is glorified both on the mountain and on the cross.

Starter

Beforehand prepare a message that they can communally discover by making a rubbing of it. (Cut out each letter of the message from cardboard and stick the letters on a card or paper base. Cover the whole thing with lining paper, secured with sticky tape.) Give everyone crayons to rub over the lining paper in order to see the message:

NOW YOU HAVE SEEN THE HIDDEN MESSAGE!

Teaching

Point out that the message was just as much there before they saw it; it was simply hidden from view. Today we are going to look at a time when God's glory became very obvious in Jesus. Read Mark's account of the Transfiguration on the mountain top. Think over what it revealed about Jesus, what it made clear and plain. (That Jesus was God's Son; he was filled with God's glory; he had God's authority; he was fulfilling the Law and the prophets; suffering and death had to be part of the rescue plan.)

How else in his life did Jesus show God's glory, but not by literally "shining" with it? (In the way he spoke and taught; the way he healed and comforted; and, above all, in being willing to die a cursed death on the cross.)

Look at what John says about this in his gospel (John 1:14).

Also read the Psalm for today, verse 3, and Exodus 3:2, Exodus 13:21, Deuteronomy 4:24, 2 Kings 2:11 and Daniel 7:9–10. Notice how the image of shining brightness and fire is seen as a sign of God's presence.

Praying

Shine, Jesus, shine,
fill this land with the Father's glory;
blaze, Spirit, blaze,
set our hearts on fire!

(From the song by Graham Kendrick
© 1987 Make Way Music)

Activities

There is space on the activity sheet to explore the references in more detail, and look at the crucifixion in terms of "the Son of Man being glorified." They can also try expressing this shining glory in a collage of words suggested on the sheet, using glowing, shining paper and foil. Have a variety of materials available.

Discussion starters

1. Think through your own areas of possessions and control which you enjoy and value. Imagine the prospect of relinquishing them, one by one. Where do you find yourself feeling instinctively possessive or protective?

2. What arguments might have been used to justify Jesus avoiding suffering and death—and why won't they hold up?

Notes

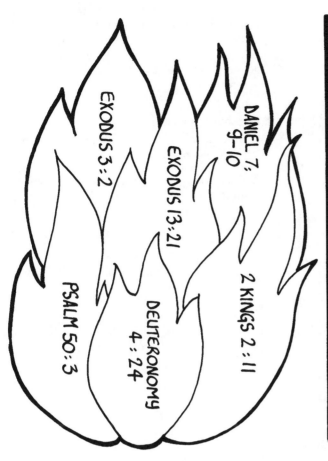

DANIEL 7: 9-10

EXODUS 3:2

EXODUS 13:21

2 KINGS 2:11

PSALM 50:3

DEUTERONOMY 4:24

ON THE MOUNTAIN

IS THERE ANY REASON WHY IT HAPPENED ON A MOUNTAIN?

Well, mountains were thought of as holy places.

BECAUSE THEY'RE HIGH, AND SET APART FROM ORDINARY LIFE?

Yes, that's right. And traditionally God had shown his glory on mountains.

DIDN'T MOSES GET THE TEN COMMANDMENTS ON A MOUNTAIN?

He did indeed.

WHY WAS JESUS SEEN TALKING WITH MOSES AND ELIJAH?

Moses represented God's Law and Elijah God's prophets. So Jesus was seen to be Messiah, fulfilling the Law and the prophets.

WRITE THE KEY WORDS AND PHRASES AROUND THE FLAMES IN THE GLORY OF GOD – USE COLOURS OF FLAME AND SHINY PAPER TO CREATE A COLLAGE OF GOD'S GLORY!

HOW COULD THIS BE CALLED GLORY?

SHINE, JESUS, SHINE,
FILL THIS LAND WITH THE FATHER'S GLORY;
BLAZE, SPIRIT, BLAZE,
SET OUR HEARTS ON FIRE!

(From the song by Graham Kendrick
© 1987 Make Way Music)

CLUES
- GOD'S GLORY IS LOVE, SHINING
- WHAT DOES THE CROSS SAY ABOUT LOVE?
- HOW CAN GOD'S GLORY SHINE IN OUR WORLD?

Third Sunday of Lent

Thought for the day

God's wisdom may shock us. Jesus, obedient to God's Law and fulfilling it, dies a death which, according to the Law, makes him cursed.

Readings

Exodus 20:1–17
1 Corinthians 1:22–25
John 2:13–25

Aim: To explore the implications of obeying God's Law.

Starter

They invent a simple ball game with clear rules, which gives everyone a chance to be involved.

Teaching

Point out the value of the rules, which make it possible for the game to be played fairly. Before you read the ten commandments from Exodus, check that they remember who is being given these rules and when. (The people of Israel, through their leader, Moses, after they had escaped from slavery in Egypt and were wandering in the wilderness.)

As each of the commandments is read (reading around the group), place cards of individual commandments on the table, together with memory joggers as described in the All-age ideas.

Draw attention to the first commandment, and discuss what they might expect God's temple to be like, in the light of this rule. You could also refer to Isaiah 56:7. Bearing those ideas in mind, read the gospel for today, so they can see how far the people had wandered from God's will as expressed in that first commandment.

How was Jesus being obedient to God's Law? When might obedience to God mean getting into trouble with the Law?

Praying

Jesus Christ is raging, raging in the streets
where injustice spirals and all hope retreats.
Listen, Lord Jesus, I am angry too;
in the kingdom's causes let me rage with you.

(Taken from the song *Jesus Christ is waiting*
by John L. Bell and Graham Maule
© 1988 WGRG, GIA Publications Inc.)

Activities

On the activity sheet there is an obedience quiz and some headline situations to get them thinking about what makes them angry "in the kingdom's causes," and what might be done about such things. The discussion may lead on to wanting active involvement in working for justice, peace and reconciliation.

Discussion starters

1. In what way is the "Law of the Lord" refreshing to us, reviving the spirit?

2. What was it about the temple that made Jesus so angry? Might he find anything in our churches to anger him?

Notes

MORE DESERT QUESTIONS

OBEDIENCE QUIZ

① You see someone struggling to get a baby stroller down a flight of steps you're walking up. Do you give them a hand?

② You know that as a Christian you should be reading the Bible regularly. Are you making an effort to do it?

③ 'Forgive our trespasses *as we forgive*.' Any outstanding forgiving to be done?

④ Is it ever OK to lie? Are you spending some time each day praying?

To MEASURE BY...

⓪ LOVE GOD: LOVE ONE ANOTHER

⑤

GETTING ANGRY

WE DON'T OFTEN SEE JESUS AS ANGRY AS THIS, DO WE?

No – you can really feel him seething as he upsets all those tables, can't you?

ISN'T IT WRONG TO BE ANGRY LIKE THAT? Losing your temper and lashing out is wrong, but we're meant to get angry at things which are very wrong – then we're inspired to put them right.

MARKETS AREN'T WRONG THOUGH, ARE THEY? Oh no! What Jesus was angry about was turning God's house into a market, when it was meant to be a house of prayer.

CHURCH LEADERS CALL FOR END TO LATEST CONFLICT

CHILDREN BRUTALLY BEATEN BY CARERS

PLANET EARTH POISONED BY ITS OWN POLLUTION

HOMELESS IN CRISIS DURING COLD SNAP

ANGRY!

WHAT MAKES YOU ANGRY IN THE KINGDOM'S CAUSES?

JESUS CHRIST IS RAGING, RAGING IN THE STREETS WHERE INJUSTICE SPIRALS AND ALL HOPE RETREATS. LISTEN, LORD JESUS, I AM ANGRY TOO; IN THE KINGDOM'S CAUSES LET ME RAGE WITH YOU.

(Taken from the song *Jesus Christ is Waiting* by John L. Bell and Graham Maule, © 1988 WGRG, GIA Publications, Inc.)

IT MAKES ME ANGRY THAT...

Fourth Sunday of Lent

Thought for the day

God loves us so much that he is generous with his mercy.

Readings

2 Chronicles 36:14–16, 19–23
Ephesians 2:4–10
John 3:14–21

Aim: To look at God's mercy and the way he sets us free, rather than condemning us.

Starter

One by one competitors sit in the hot seat and try to keep a perfectly straight face, while everyone else (from a short distance away) endeavors to make them smile. Have ready a whoopee cushion or some other sound effect to use for announcing that a player is out of the game.

Teaching

As soon as we broke the "no smiling" rule we were out, with no mercy shown and no second chance in that round. When people break the rules in society the whoopee cushion for them is the charge brought against them and the sentence they are given. If they are condemned, is mercy shown to them? Our legal system was founded on Christian principles. We do have the possibility of mercy, in such things as being granted bail, remission for good behavior and the right to appeal.

What about when we break God's law of love? Read together the passage from Chronicles, noticing God's mercy and patience as his people continue to break the law of love, in spite of the help they are sent again and again. Their law-breaking is bound to end them in national disaster; by insisting on following evil they bring it on themselves. Talk about the way it seems to be human nature to do this— we aren't able to do the good we know we should, and all too often we end up doing the opposite. That means that we all break the law of love, and deserve God's condemnation.

Now read today's gospel. What does Jesus say? Was he sent into the world to condemn us in a massive clean-up operation? No, he wasn't sent to condemn but so that through him the world might be saved.

Finally read the passage from Ephesians. Paul realizes that we can't sort it out for ourselves. It's certain that we can't. But grace is a different matter. Grace is God's freely given love which we can't earn, but we *can* accept. In accepting, we are show-ing that we put our trust in Jesus.

Praying

O most merciful Redeemer, friend and brother,
may we know you more clearly
love you more dearly
and follow you more nearly
day by day. Amen.

(From St. Richard of Chichester's prayer)

Activities

On the activity sheet there is a mixture of condemning and mercy vocabulary to sort and read out, so that the contrast alerts us to the true nature of God. They also look at what we mean by "grace" in relation to God's mercy.

Discussion starters

1. Have we allowed Jesus to deal with any areas of condemnation in our own lives? Do we really believe he can?

2. Why doesn't God give up on us?

Notes

CONDEMNATION

DESPAIR
ENCOURAGEMENT
LOVE KINDNESS CRUSHING
REJECTION
PUNISHMENT OR PATIENCE HOPELESSNESS
HOPE
JUDGEMENT ACCUSATION UNDERSTANDING
FORGIVENESS

MERCY

SORT OUT WHICH WORDS ARE WHICH

READ OUT ALL THE CONDEMNATION WORDS ...

... AND THEN ALL THE MERCY WORDS

NOT CONDEMNATION BUT MERCY

IT'S TERRIBLE TO THINK OF BEING CONDEMNED – AS IF ALL HOPE IS LOCKED OUT AND YOU'RE LOCKED IN .

Yes, I agree. Even if you know you've done a terrible wrong, being condemned is the end of hope.

I SUPPOSE IF WE'RE DESIGNED TO LOVE GOD AND LOVE ONE ANOTHER, GOD HAS EVERY REASON TO CONDEMN US, LOOKING AT OUR TRACK RECORD .

That's true. But as God's whole nature is LOVE, he doesn't condemn us. He has mercy on us instead.

JUST AS WELL ! HE MUST HAVE AMAZING LOVE TO DO THAT .

Yes – total, complete loving!

IT IS GOD'S NATURE TO HAVE MERCY

GOD'S GRACE IS LIKE A FREELY GIVEN GIFT

* WE CAN'T BUY IT
* WE CAN'T EARN IT
* WE CAN RECEIVE IT !

O MOST MERCIFUL REDEEMER,
FRIEND AND BROTHER,
MAY WE KNOW YOU MORE CLEARLY,
LOVE YOU MORE DEARLY,
AND FOLLOW YOU MORE NEARLY
DAY BY DAY.
— AMEN —
(FROM ST RICHARD OF CHICHESTER'S PRAYER)

Fifth Sunday of Lent

Thought for the day

Through Christ's death, full life would come to people of all nations and generations.

Readings

Jeremiah 31:31–34
Hebrews 5:7–9
John 12:20–33

Aim: To look at the significance of the Gentiles coming to Jesus and hearing his teaching at this point.

Starter

Have some blotting paper and dampen it so they can watch a spot of color from various dark-colored markers spreading out in all directions and revealing lots of hidden colors.

Teaching

Have the spreading blots displayed as you read the passage from Jeremiah, focusing on the opening-up of people's knowledge of God: "…all of them will know me, says the Lord." Go on to look at John 12:20–22. As this gospel is very condensed, it's best to take it in sections.

Explain that the Greeks were Gentiles, and John wants us to know that here are representatives from the "other nations" seeking Jesus out. Take them briefly back to the wedding at Cana (John 2:3–5) where Jesus had said his hour had not yet come, and then read what Jesus says when he finds these Gentiles looking for him (John 12:23). Everyone can read this verse aloud together. This is the point in Jesus' ministry when the "stand by for action" lights start flashing. The big act of total self-giving has moved from the long-term planning stage to red alert, and, humanly speaking, Jesus' adrenaline starts pumping.

As he starts teaching them about what to expect (John 12:24–26), all the horror of what it will entail rushes into him, and John gives us a blow-by-blow account of Jesus, the Son of God, wrestling with the human temptation to scream, "Stop! I can't go through with it!" (verse 27). What will happen? Wonderfully, Jesus manages to triumph in that battle, and chooses for God's name to be glorified, whatever the cost to himself (verse 28a).

We can imagine God the Father on the edge of his seat (so to speak) through Jesus' agonizing, and now immediately he is there to affirm and comfort him, giving him a new surge of confidence, which we can hear in Jesus' voice in the last couple of verses (28b–33).

Praying

Father, may your name be glorified!
Whatever the cost,
may your will be done in me.

Activities

On the activity sheet they can trace the way Jesus has to go through this human temptation so that the self-giving is freely chosen, in full knowledge of the cost involved. This commitment is then related to their own lives and faith journey. They are also helped to see how the grain of wheat analogy works.

Discussion starters

1. How does it help that even Jesus shrank from the thought of the suffering ahead?

2. How is it that Jesus being lifted up (both when crucified and ascended) can draw all humanity to himself?

Notes

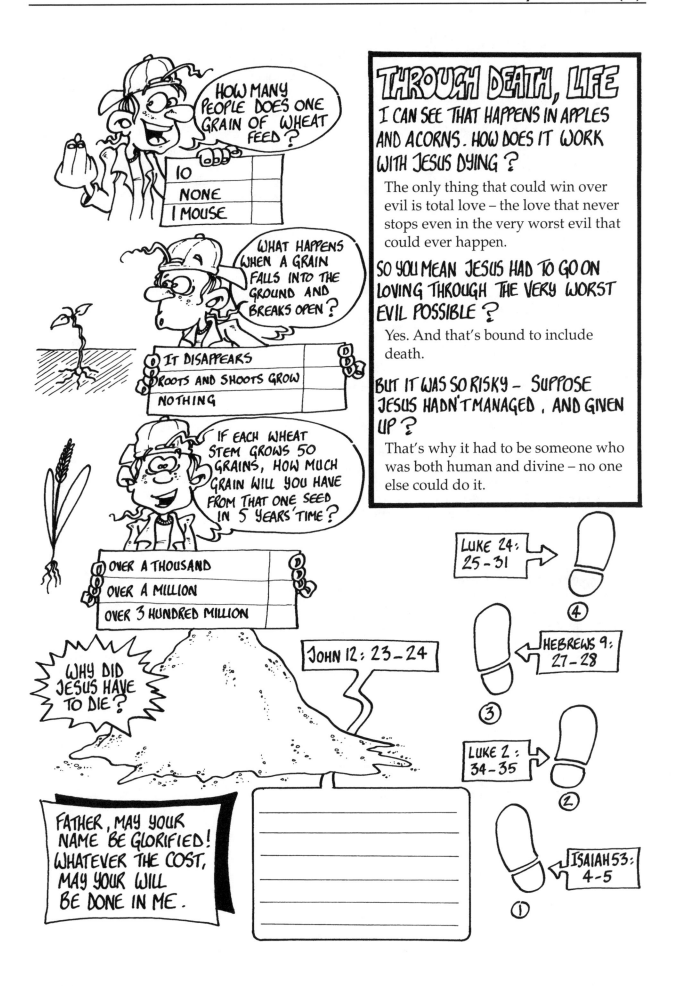

Holy Week

Passion (Palm) Sunday

Thought for the day

As the Messiah, Jesus enters Jerusalem, knowing that he rides towards rejection and death in order to save his people.

Readings

Liturgy of the Palms:
Mark 11:1–10 or John 12:12–16

Liturgy of the Passion:
Isaiah 50:4–7
Philippians 2:6–11
Mark 14:1—15:47 or Mark 15:1–39 (40–47)

Aim: To look at why the Messiah had to suffer and die before he could rise in glory.

Starter

If possible, let the young people join in with the all-age procession, playing instruments, and carrying banners as they go. Or gather all the age groups and take them on a Palm Sunday procession, preferably outside. The banners read "Jesus is the Christ" and "Jesus is the Messiah."

Teaching

Remind everyone of the way the prophets had known for many generations that God would one day send his chosen One, like a new King David, to save his people and reign forever. The image they had of this Savior was not all riding out to battle with the occupying army. Read from Isaiah 50, which is one of the passages about the suffering servant, noticing how the prophet senses the need for the Savior to be despised and rejected as part of his saving work of love.

Notice the links with the story of the Passion, where we see Jesus in this suffering servant role (Mark 14:1—15:47). Read the Passion with different voices for the different parts, with everyone reading the crowd parts. It is worthwhile to spend time on this.

Praying

Father's pure radiance, perfect in innocence,
yet learns obedience to death on a cross.
Suffering to give us life,
conquering through sacrifice,
and as they crucify prays: "Father, forgive."

O what a mystery, meekness and majesty.
Bow down and worship,
for this is your God.

(Taken from the song *Meekness and Majesty* by Graham Kendrick © 1986 Kingsway's Thankyou Music/EMI Christian Music Publishing)

Activities

There is space on the activity sheet this week to express the entry into Jerusalem with its welcome and praise, but with the shadow of the cross and its painful glory present.

Discussion starters

1. What do we discover about God's nature through the events of the Passion?

2. Why did the work of saving humanity have to end like this?

Notes

FATHER'S PURE RADIANCE, PERFECT IN INNOCENCE, YET LEARNS OBEDIENCE TO DEATH ON A CROSS. SUFFERING TO GIVE US LIFE, CONQUERING THROUGH SACRIFICE, AND AS THEY CRUCIFY PRAYS: 'FATHER FORGIVE'. O WHAT A MYSTERY, MEEKNESS AND MAJESTY. BOW DOWN AND WORSHIP, FOR THIS IS YOUR GOD.

(Taken from the song *Meekness and Majesty* by Graham Kendrick © 1986 Kingsway's Thankyou Music/EMI Christian Music Publishing)

HOSANNA!

WHY WERE THE CROWDS SO EXCITED?

They badly wanted to be free, and here was the Messiah coming into their city to be their king and lead them to freedom.

BUT JESUS WASN'T THAT SORT OF KING, WAS HE? I CAN'T IMAGINE HIM LEADING AN ARMY.

Exactly. His kingdom is not about one country. It's about the hearts of people being ruled by selfless love.

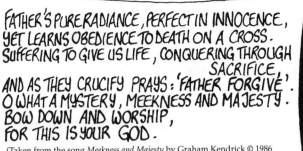

DRAW HOW THE ENTRY INTO JERUSALEM MUST HAVE FELT FOR JESUS, KNOWING WHAT WAS BOUND TO HAPPEN TO HIM —

— BE AS REALISTIC OR ABSTRACT AS YOU LIKE, TO EXPRESS THE FEELINGS!

WARFF!

Easter

Easter Day

Thought for the day
Jesus is alive; God's love has won the victory over sin and death.

Readings
Acts 10:34, 37–43
Colossians 3:1–4
John 20:1–9

Aim: To look at the accounts of the Resurrection and weigh up the evidence.

Starter
Spread out a whole pack of cards and ask one person to choose a card, without giving away which one is chosen. The rest of you are going to detect the right card by a process of elimination. The card chooser can only answer everyone's questions with a "Yes" or "No." As each question is answered, turn over all the cards now eliminated, until the correct card is there, plain to see.

Teaching
As we are used to celebrating Easter every year, the shock and impossibility of the event can get glossed over and taken for granted. As you read the gospel account today, ask them to imagine they are particular characters (tell them which before you read) so that during the reading they are thinking through that person's head. Afterwards talk to everyone in character about how they felt, and how their feelings changed.

The reading from Acts will give extra insight into Peter's character, as this is his own later account of what happened, once he's had plenty of time to think things over. Has his conviction changed or is he still convinced that Jesus is alive?

Talk over the possibilities of what really happened. It's important that these are looked at and not assumed to be rubbish. Could Jesus have not really died, but just collapsed and later recovered? Could the disciples have stolen the body? Could the disciples and the women have wanted to see Jesus and so imagined they saw him?

Look at these questions in the light of the accounts they have read, so they can see that the strange truth is actually more likely. (*Who Moved the Stone?* by Frank Morison, Bromley, 1983, can be recommended for any wanting to read further.) The facts and circumstances point to Jesus dying and rising to new life. What does that say about who Jesus was? And is?

Praying
The dead One lives
and the power of death is broken
by the power of Love.
O my Lord, this is an amazing truth,
and you are an amazing God!

Activities
There is a role-play to explore the thinking and fears of the disciples, and some information about the Resurrection events. They are encouraged to think about the difference a crucified and risen Christ makes to the way we spend the rest of our own life.

Discussion starters
1. What did the disciples gain from seeing Jesus after the Resurrection?

2. Since the Resurrection, Jesus is alive for all time, including today. Do we still tend to think of him in history? What evidence have we that Jesus is with us now?

Notes

Second Sunday of Easter

Thought for the day

Our faith in the risen Christ is bound to affect the way we live.

Readings

Acts 4:32–35
1 John 5:1–6
John 20:19–31

Aim: To look at the stages of Thomas' journey to faith.

Starter

Give small groups clues to where the different components of a flashlight are. Each group races to be the first to assemble and turn on their flashlight. (Or you could have a tape player, lead, socket and tape to assemble.)

Teaching

Our flashlights only lit up once we had gathered all the pieces and fitted them together. That's also how Inspector Morse or any other detective works. Our questions and investigations help us put facts and experiences together to reach a conclusion. Today we watch this happening in Thomas, one of the disciples who very much wanted to believe Jesus was risen, but found it very difficult. Read today's gospel. Faced with the impossibility of death turning into risen life, what makes Thomas believe?

Working with the text, go through the stages:

1. For some reason Thomas was not with the others—denial and avoidance strategy.

2. Thomas hears the stories of the others—witnesses heard.

3. Can it be true?—wavers but digs in to avoid being conned and insists on solid evidence.

4. Thomas joins the disciples same place, same time, a week later—takes a risk and puts himself in right place just in case.

5. Meets Jesus—finds that the meeting is more convincing than anything, solid proof no longer needed.

Finally read the passage from Acts to hear the faith in action.

Praying

Lord God, you hear my questions and my doubts—
they are all part of me seeking you;
lead me to a deeper understanding
of who you are and where we are going together.
Amen.

Activities

On the activity sheet there is a pictorial look at the early church and how it showed Jesus' risen life. They are also helped to look at that breathing of "beyond death" life, and how it still changes us now.

Discussion starters

1. Jesus breathes on his disciples the life that death cannot touch, the life of God's fullness. How does that change them?

2. What would you point to as evidence that Jesus is alive today, even though we cannot actually see him?

Notes

Third Sunday of Easter

Thought for the day

Having redeemed us by his death, Jesus can offer us the forgiveness of our sin, which sets us free to live.

Readings

Acts 3:13–15, 17–19
1 John 2:1–5
Luke 24:35–48

Aim: To see the importance of spreading the news of forgiveness.

Starter

Cut out news headlines from their stories, and stick them around the room separately. Everyone goes around matching up the headline with the story.

Teaching

Begin with the gospel—Luke's account of that Sunday evening encounter with the risen Jesus. Notice the similarities with last week's account, seeing how there is real fear registered at first, which Jesus carefully addresses. He doesn't even start telling them anything important until he is sure they are happy and at peace with him being there. It's the same now. We need to get used to spending quality time in Jesus' company if we are wanting him to help us understand things in life.

Now look at the passage from Acts, putting it briefly in context of the healing, and the crowd's enthusiasm to give Peter and John all the credit for it. Notice how they use the occasion to do what Jesus had told them to—telling people to change their lives, making them right with God and being set free by his forgiveness.

Finally look at the reading from 1 John, where the writer is still amazed and overjoyed by the way God's love changes lives. Again, the new life is tied up with whatever happens to us when we repent and are forgiven. It's something so good that it needs to be thoroughly investigated!

Praying

The King is among us, his Spirit is here,
let's draw near and worship, let songs fill the air.

(Taken from a song by Graham Kendrick,
© 1981 Kingsway's Thankyou Music/EMI Christian Music Publishing)

Activities

On the activity sheet they unpack the steps Jesus goes through to sort out the disciples, and the steps Peter goes through to sort out the way the crowd is thinking. They are encouraged to look at situations where we can choose to pocket the glory ourselves rather than giving it to God. There is also a look at taking up Jesus' commission to tell others the good news of forgiveness.

Discussion starters

1. Do we pass over serious, regular repentance, thinking of it only being really necessary for a few "heavyweight" sins that we haven't committed?

2. Does living the risen life feel different, as the apostles claim? If it doesn't, could it be we aren't living it yet?

Notes

Fourth Sunday of Easter

Thought for the day

"I am the Good Shepherd and I lay down my life for the sheep."

Readings

Acts 4:8–12
1 John 3:1–2
John 10:11–18

Aim: To look at how Jesus takes on himself the role of the Good Shepherd.

Starter

Role-call. Give out identities to particular people, which they keep secret. Then provide a situation which they all act out in role. Onlookers have to guess the identities/characters from the way they are acting. (Example: travelling on a train, someone with chicken pox, a spy, a newspaper reporter looking for a story, and the President travelling incognito.)

Teaching

Jesus knew the Scriptures and what had been written about the Messiah in the books of the prophets, and the Psalms. There was quite a lot about God's shepherding (read Psalm 23) and the Messiah would be a kind of Shepherd King, like David. (Have a look at a few examples, such as 2 Samuel 5:2; Psalm 28:9; Ezekiel 34:16; Isaiah 40:11.) There was also a recurring theme of the false shepherding of God's people, who were left as sheep without a shepherd (Ezekiel 34:5). In Mark and Matthew, Jesus is said to have compassion on the people because of this (Matthew 9:36 and Mark 6:34).

Often the leaders of God's people are criticized for their unshepherdlike behavior (Jeremiah 10:21; Ezekiel 34:2; Isaiah 56:11).

So now, with this background, look at today's gospel, John 10:11–18. Jesus is not only showing his disciples the example of the real shepherds around on the hills where they were living. He is also directing them to see how he is fulfilling the prophets and the Psalms as the real, authentic leader of God's people, in contrast to those who are only out for themselves, and are not listening carefully to God.

Praying

The Lord is my shepherd; I shall not want.
He makes me lie down in green pastures
and leads me beside still waters.
He revives my soul
and guides me along right pathways
for his name's sake.
Though I walk through the valley
of the shadow of death,
I shall fear no evil;
for you are with me;
your rod and your staff comfort me.
You spread a table for me
in the sight of those who trouble me;
you have anointed my head with oil,
and my cup is running over.
Surely your goodness and mercy shall follow me
all the days of my life,
and I will dwell in the house of the Lord forever.

(Psalm 23)

Activities

On the activity sheet there is a picture of a hired shepherd fleeing in danger, and they are helped to explore this symbol in terms of leadership of God's people, and our own Christian witness. They are also introduced to the full story in Acts (chapter 4, verses 2–12) of Peter and John putting themselves in danger for the sake of the gospel, so that they can see how this links in with Jesus laying down his life for the sheep.

Discussion starters

1. Does our lack of trust in the Good Shepherd and our lack of expectation prevent his work being done?

2. How has God redeemed unpromising events in your life (as individuals and as a church) and turned them into good opportunities?

Notes

GULP – I'M OFF!

Why are Israel's spiritual leaders accused of being like this?

Jeremiah 10:21
Ezekiel 34:2
Isaiah 56:11

BAAAA!!!

GOTCHA!

How does our own Christian caring measure up?

They might tease me.

I don't want to look silly.

I need all my money to spend on me!

I want a nice, easy life.

"I AM THE GOOD SHEPHERD"

WHY DID JESUS SAY HE WAS THE 'GOOD' SHEPHERD? All those listening to Jesus knew that only the shepherds who really cared for the sheep would bother to take risks for them.

AND JESUS IS A RISK-TAKING SHEPHERD? Yes. Jesus knows us really well, and loves us.

WHAT ABOUT LAYING DOWN HIS LIFE FOR US – IT SOUNDS AS IF JESUS COULD HAVE CHOSEN NOT TO BE KILLED. That's right. He could have called on all heaven's powers to get down from that cross and walk away.

BUT THEN HE WOULDN'T HAVE SAVED US, WOULD HE? No.

THE LORD IS MY SHEPHERD; I SHALL NOT BE IN WANT.
HE MAKES ME LIE DOWN IN GREEN PASTURES
AND LEADS ME BESIDE STILL WATERS.
HE REVIVES MY SOUL AND GUIDES ME ALONG RIGHT
PATHWAYS FOR HIS NAME'S SAKE.
THOUGH I WALK THROUGH THE VALLEY OF THE SHADOW
OF DEATH I SHALL FEAR NO EVIL;
FOR YOU ARE WITH ME; YOUR ROD AND YOUR STAFF
COMFORT ME.
YOU SPREAD A TABLE FOR ME IN THE SIGHT
OF THOSE WHO TROUBLE ME;
YOU HAVE ANOINTED MY HEAD WITH OIL,
AND MY CUP IS RUNNING OVER.
SURELY YOUR GOODNESS AND MERCY SHALL
FOLLOW ME ALL THE DAYS OF MY LIFE,
AND I WILL DWELL IN THE HOUSE OF THE LORD
FOR EVER.

– PSALM 23 –

BECAUSE THEY WERE TELLING EVERYONE THAT...

WHY WERE PETER AND JOHN IN PRISON?

ACTS 4: 2-12

Fifth Sunday of Easter

Thought for the day
To produce fruit we need to be joined onto the true vine.

Readings
Acts 9:26–31
1 John 3:18–24
John 15:1–8

Aim: To understand the importance of us being "joined on" to Jesus if we are to produce any fruit spiritually.

Starter
Have a small set of Christmas tree lights and arrange it so that it has one "bad" bulb. Show how they are all linked together, and how they won't light up because of the one "bad" bulb. Replace the bulb with a good one and show how they are all lit from the same source.

Teaching
We all enjoy being free to do the things we like doing and don't like it when anyone cramps our style or tries to restrict our freedom. Left entirely free, a vine plant will grow like any other creeper—all over the place; it may have a good free time but the grapes will scarcely be worth bothering with. If tied to some sort of frame and carefully pruned, the same vine will be much more productive and the grapes could be well on the way to becoming a famous vintage.

List some of the ways in which we are "pruned" in ordinary activities, where our freedom to do what we like may be limited but for a good reason and with, hopefully, good results. (Things like sports training, music practice, getting a good night's sleep, even the rules of the games we play.)

Read the passage from John's gospel. How can we make sure that we are part of the true vine? In what ways do other aspects of our lives need pruning?

Praying
Breathe on me, Breath of God,
fill me with life anew,
that I may love what thou dost love,
and do what thou wouldst do.

Activities
They are encouraged to check their own position on (or off) the true vine, reviewing how their practice matches up with where they want to be. They are also introduced to Barnabas and his distinctive ministry of encouragement.

Discussion starters
1. How can we check that we are still firmly attached to the true vine?

2. Does belonging to the true vine mean that we have to sacrifice our independence?

Notes

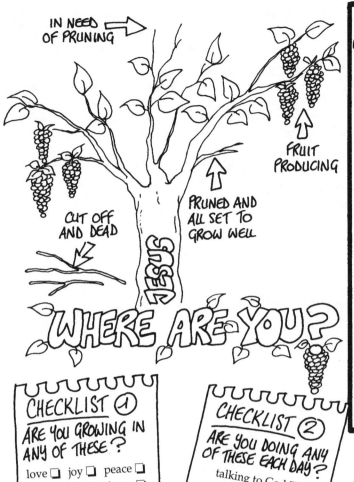

IN NEED OF PRUNING →

FRUIT PRODUCING

PRUNED AND ALL SET TO GROW WELL

CUT OFF AND DEAD

JESUS

WHERE ARE YOU?

I AM THE TRUE VINE

IS THAT ANOTHER WAY OF SAYING 'LIVE IN ME AND I WILL LIVE IN YOU'?

Yes. It's a good picture of the way Jesus' life fills our life, so that we can live lovingly.

SO JESUS NEEDS US AS WELL AS US NEEDING HIM?

That's right. We work together. Your words and hands and feet can bring God's love to the places *you* go and the people *you* meet.

WHAT IF WE TRY TO GO IT ALONE?

Soon the stocks run out. That's why we need to be joined on to the living supply which keeps renewing and refilling us.

CHECKLIST ①
ARE YOU GROWING IN ANY OF THESE?

love ☐   joy ☐   peace ☐
patience ☐   kindness ☐
goodness ☐
faithfulness ☐
gentleness ☐
self-control ☐

CHECKLIST ②
ARE YOU DOING ANY OF THESE EACH DAY?

talking to God ☐
listening to God ☐
wanting to live God's way ☐
reading your Bible ☐
thanking God ☐

WHY WERE THE APOSTLES IN JERUSALEM AFRAID OF PAUL?

BREATHE ON ME, BREATH OF GOD,
FILL ME WITH LIFE ANEW,
THAT I MAY LOVE
WHAT THOU DOST LOVE,
AND DO
WHAT THOU WOULDST DO.

HOW DID BARNABAS HELP PAUL?

_____
_____
_____

WHAT CAN WE LEARN FROM THE WAY BARNABAS BEHAVED?

_____
_____
_____

Sixth Sunday of Easter

Thought for the day
We are to love one another as Jesus loves us.

Readings
Acts 10:25–26, 34–35, 44–48
1 John 4:7–10
John 15:9–17

Aim: To look at what it means to be Jesus' friends.

Starter
Either use the sketch found on p. 126, or play a cooperative game such as making a circle of everyone sitting on the lap of the person in front, or telling a story in which each person in the circle adds a word.

Teaching
Begin by reading today's gospel, which follows last week's picture of the vine and branches. Bear in mind when Jesus was saying these things—shortly before his arrest and death. Ask them to pick out particular phrases that seem specially important, or which surprise them. Being Jesus' friends looks as if it brings both honor and responsibility. What are these? (That we have the privilege of working cooperatively with the living God; that we are to love one another as Jesus loves us.)

Now look at 1 John 4:7–10, particularly verses 7–8. Make it clear that we do not love God in order for him to like us. It's God's love for us which makes us love him and want to live like him.

Finally look at an example of cooperative friendship with Jesus—Peter going along with God's will even though it's not what he might have chosen to do on his own, with the result that all those people receive the Holy Spirit and the freedom that gives.

Praying
(To pray regularly throughout each day)

Here I am, Lord,
ready to work with you.
Show me how I can share your love
here…now.

Activities
On the activity sheet they are helped to explore how Jesus loves us, and what that is going to mean for us loving one another. They are also looking at the way we are chosen and appointed to go and bear fruit—both the honor and the responsibility.

Discussion starters
1. Jesus once observed that it is those who have been forgiven much who love much. Do we feel fully forgiven, with the rush of love that produces, or has the penny yet to drop?

2. Imagine walking through a normal day, meeting the usual people and problems, but in the knowledge of God's love and forgiveness, and literally loving as Jesus loves us. What would it be like, and how would it differ from how we usually live?

Notes

Seventh Sunday of Easter

Thought for the day

Although now hidden from our sight, Jesus lives forever, and in him we can live the Resurrection life even while we are on earth.

Readings

Acts 1:15–17, 20–26
1 John 4:11–16
John 17:11–19

Aim: To look at what it means to live in Jesus and live the risen life.

Starter

Two teams (or more for larger numbers) sit facing each other, about a yard apart. The aim is to hit a balloon behind the other team's chairs.

Teaching

If no one has been involved in Ascension, include it now by starting the Acts reading from verse 9. Point out that Peter feels it is a matter of urgency to choose a replacement for Judas, and part of their preparation for receiving the gift of the Holy Spirit. They are putting everything in order, ready for the new life. Notice, too, how God's choice is what matters, not anyone else's. We can learn from this to get our lives facing the right direction in readiness for God to act in them, and actively to want God's will in all the choices and decisions we make each day.

Now read John 17:6–19. Jesus is praying for all of us who live as his followers in the world, knowing how difficult it will sometimes be for us, but not praying for us to be taken out of the dangers because the work we are doing is so vital; it needs doing. It is reassuring for us to know that whenever we are talking about our faith, or standing up for what is right, or helping someone else to think through their faith, Jesus is there praying for us and, through him, God's life is there in us, giving us the words to say, and the courage to do the work.

Praying

O come to my heart, Lord Jesus,
there is room in my heart for thee.

Activities

On the activity sheet they are encouraged to join the disciples in their waiting on God during this coming week, asking for a fresh outpouring of the Holy Spirit. And they are helped to look at any preparation in their own lives that needs to be done.

Discussion starters

1. In what way are we "one," in spite of the different labels and packaging?
2. How can we, who live two thousand years after Christ, be considered "witnesses"?

Notes

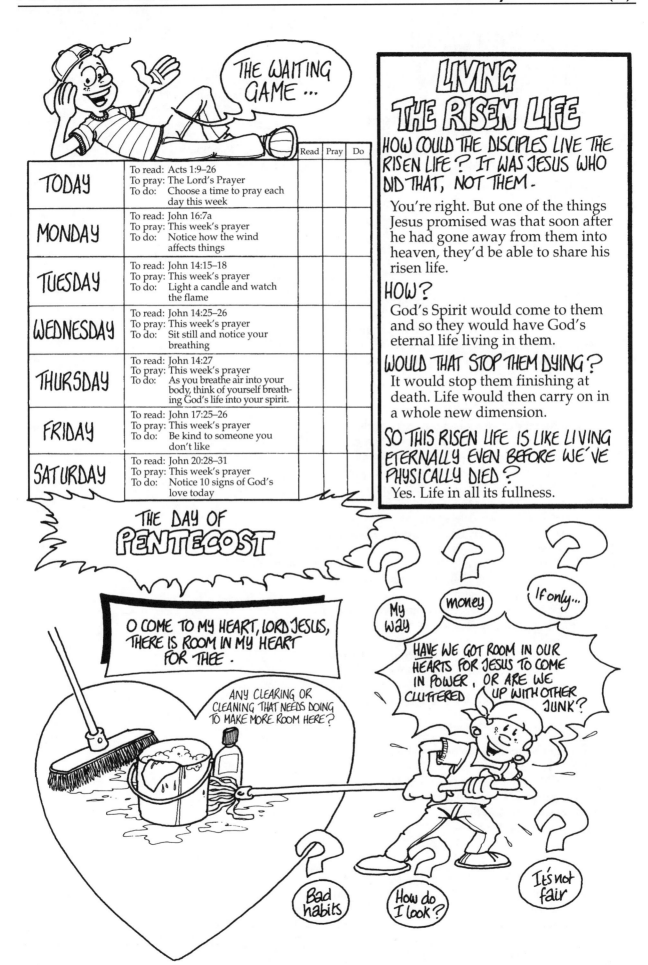

THE WAITING GAME …

		Read	Pray	Do
TODAY	To read: Acts 1:9–26 To pray: The Lord's Prayer To do: Choose a time to pray each day this week			
MONDAY	To read: John 16:7a To pray: This week's prayer To do: Notice how the wind affects things			
TUESDAY	To read: John 14:15–18 To pray: This week's prayer To do: Light a candle and watch the flame			
WEDNESDAY	To read: John 14:25–26 To pray: This week's prayer To do: Sit still and notice your breathing			
THURSDAY	To read: John 14:27 To pray: This week's prayer To do: As you breathe air into your body, think of yourself breathing God's life into your spirit.			
FRIDAY	To read: John 17:25–26 To pray: This week's prayer To do: Be kind to someone you don't like			
SATURDAY	To read: John 20:28–31 To pray: This week's prayer To do: Notice 10 signs of God's love today			

THE DAY OF PENTECOST

LIVING THE RISEN LIFE

HOW COULD THE DISCIPLES LIVE THE RISEN LIFE? IT WAS JESUS WHO DID THAT, NOT THEM.

You're right. But one of the things Jesus promised was that soon after he had gone away from them into heaven, they'd be able to share his risen life.

HOW?

God's Spirit would come to them and so they would have God's eternal life living in them.

WOULD THAT STOP THEM DYING?

It would stop them finishing at death. Life would then carry on in a whole new dimension.

SO THIS RISEN LIFE IS LIKE LIVING ETERNALLY EVEN BEFORE WE'VE PHYSICALLY DIED?

Yes. Life in all its fullness.

O COME TO MY HEART, LORD JESUS, THERE IS ROOM IN MY HEART FOR THEE.

ANY CLEARING OR CLEANING THAT NEEDS DOING TO MAKE MORE ROOM HERE?

My way

money

If only…

HAVE WE GOT ROOM IN OUR HEARTS FOR JESUS TO COME IN POWER, OR ARE WE CLUTTERED UP WITH OTHER JUNK?

Bad habits

How do I look?

It's not fair

Pentecost

Thought for the day
The Holy Spirit of God is poured out in power on the expectant disciples, just as Jesus promised.

Readings
Acts 2:1–11
1 Corinthians 12:3–7, 12–13
John 20:19–23

Aim: To look at how the coming of the Holy Spirit affected the disciples and affects Jesus' followers now.

Starter
All change! Have a selection of scarves and hats, enough for everyone and as silly as you like. Use a CD player for music so that you can skip from track to track. When the music starts, each person dresses up. Whenever the track changes, they have to swap their hat and scarf with someone else.

Teaching
Explain that the disciples had seen a lot of changes in the last few years of their lives. Jesus had called them out of their normal jobs, they'd travelled around to different places, changed their way of thinking and their way of thinking about God. They'd lived through the crucifixion, Jesus being dead and Jesus being alive again. Now they were waiting for another change, not quite knowing what the Holy Spirit would do to them, but knowing it was important to be ready for it.

Now read from Acts. Consider having this reading prepared on tape, either from a professional recording, or using a couple of adults from the congregation, and adding the sound of the wind, or some music.

What has happened to the disciples with the coming of the Holy Spirit? How are they behaving? How are they different? Why are they so excited? What was it they wanted everyone to know?

Praying
Lord, that power the disciples were given—
I want it, too.
I've seen the way they were changed
and strengthened—and I want that, too.
Will you let your Holy Spirit
come to me and fill my life?

Activities
There is a short sketch to start them looking at the possibility of the Holy Spirit changing things still, today and here. And they are encouraged to learn how to wait on God, both privately and as a group,

Discussion starters
1. Why isn't the Holy Spirit poured out more than it is in our own church? What can we learn from the disciples' expectant waiting?

2. Do we try to impose restrictions or guidelines for the Holy Spirit in case our lives are too much challenged by too much of God's presence?

Notes

THE HOLY SPIRIT OF GOD

WHAT REALLY HAPPENED? WAS THERE A STORM WITH LIGHTNING OR SOMETHING?

Those who were there said it sounded like a rushing wind and they sensed brightness rather like flames. But it was not actual wind and fire. The onlookers came running to see what had happened.

I SUPPOSE GOD'S POWER IS BOUND TO BE SPECTACULAR LIKE THAT.

Not always. Sometimes the Spirit comes very gently, giving a sense of deep peace and calm.

CAN THE HOLY SPIRIT STILL COME TO US TODAY?

It can and it does!

Beth: Have you noticed how Dave's changed over the last few months?

Ryan: Yes, I have. He seems more settled. And he doesn't keep losing his temper.

Carl: He lost it last week though.

Ryan: Yeah, but that was when he got mad at Ross for kicking my shirt into the gutter.

Beth: In the old days it would have been Dave doing the shirt kicking!

Carl: What's happened?

Ryan: Well, we've all been praying for him, haven't we? And he's been asking questions about things as well.

Beth: What things?

Ryan: Oh, you know—who made God . . . what are ghosts . . . that kind of stuff.

Carl: God's amazing. Imagine him listening to our prayers.

Beth: Yes, and he's sorting Dave out. God's power is so incredible.

All: God does things. God ACTS TOO.

Carl: Acts 2! That's today's reading!

HOW TO GET IN ON THE ACTS!

Learn how to wait on the living, real God, making yourself still and quiet, and attentive.

Expect God to act.

Read the book of Acts straight through, to see God at work in his friends.

Want God's kingdom to come and God's will to be done.

Live thankfully.

LORD, THAT POWER THE DISCIPLES WERE GIVEN— I WANT IT, TOO. I'VE SEEN THE WAY THEY WERE CHANGED AND STRENGTHENED— AND I WANT THAT, TOO. WILL YOU LET YOUR HOLY SPIRIT COME TO ME AND FILL MY LIFE?

Feasts of the Lord

Trinity Sunday

Thought for the day

The mysterious and holy nature of the one true God is beyond our understanding, but it is both communal harmony and individual personality, Father, Son and Holy Spirit.

Readings

Deuteronomy 4:32–34, 39–40
Romans 8:14–17
Matthew 28:16–20

Aim: To explore the nature of the Trinity.

Starter

Who are you? The group is going to discover as much as possible about you in five minutes. Before the timing starts, let them collectively establish what they do know about you already, so the question time isn't wasted. Explain that if you don't want to answer a particular question you will say so; but they can ask whatever they want to in order to get to know who you are and what you are like.

Teaching

Look back at how the group discovered more about you. They ran their minds over what they knew already and went on from there. Were there some things they thought they knew that turned out to be mistaken? Were they surprised by any of the new discoveries?

Today, on Trinity Sunday, we are focusing on who God is and what he is like. Collectively as a church, over the years, some clear truths about God have been discovered:

• God is One Being

• God is Three Persons—Father, Son and Holy Spirit.

(Trinity means Tri-Unity, or Three in One and One in Three.)

Why does the church describe God in this way? Look together at what they know of God as Father, Son and Spirit, to see how the concept of Trinity has developed, referring to these passages to help: Genesis 1:1–3; Isaiah 9:6; Luke 1:35; John 10:36–38; John 14:25–26; and John 3:1–17 where the invisible nature of the wind helps Nicodemus discover more about the nature of God.

Praying

Holy, holy, holy is the Lord Almighty;

the whole earth is full of his glory!

Activities

On the activity sheet there are aspects of the natural world which can help us understand more about the nature of God: the wind; infinity of space; simplicity/complexity of life structures; light; physical laws and order.

Discussion starters

1. How does each Person of the Trinity testify to the others?

2. What would you like God to enable you to "see"?

Notes

Ordinary Time

Second Sunday in Ordinary Time

Thought for the day
Christ calls us to follow him and walk his way through our lifetime.

Readings
1 Samuel 3:3–10, 19
1 Corinthians 6:13–15, 17–20
John 1:35–42

Aim: To look at vocation and our response.

Starter
Give out a circled job advertisement in a newspaper, and prepare three or four simple profiles to give the applicants, including such facts as age, qualifications and experience. The rest of the group are the panel interviewing them for the job, and they decide which one to appoint.

Teaching
When God calls people for particular jobs he already knows all about them, and knows they will be perfectly suited to the work he is calling them to. (That's why it's such a sensible idea to consult God when we are thinking about jobs we might do.) But when God calls, it doesn't always look like what we were hoping to do.

Read the passage from 1 Samuel, pointing out that at first Samuel hadn't been trained by Eli to listen for God's call, and three times it took for Eli to realize that it was God who had been calling Samuel. Then the message Samuel was given wasn't a nice comforting one but one saying very unpleasant things about Eli and his sons, so Samuel didn't at first want to tell Eli what God had said. Bravely he told him, and went on to become a really good shepherd of God's people.

Now look at the calling of the first disciples in today's gospel. Andrew and his friend are ready and alert to take notice of what John the Baptist tells them about Jesus, and they make a point of seeking Jesus' company. Simon Peter is dragged along to meet Jesus by the enthusiasm of his brother Andrew, and so it goes on. Something in Jesus makes them sure that this wild and crazy idea of following a wandering preacher is a good one, if unusual and unexpected. They can feel how important it is, even though as yet they don't exactly know why.

When God calls us, he doesn't lay all the details

out right away. He just lodges the conviction in us that we have to follow him in a particular direction, and, as we start to follow, the next bit of the job becomes clearer. He invites, but never pressures. If, like Samuel, we don't recognize his call the first time, he'll wait to get our attention again, and then quietly repeat the same call. If we agree to follow, he'll set off and expect us to keep up with him. Those first disciples were probably surprised it happened to be they who were called; we shouldn't be too surprised if we find God calling us!

Praying
Here I am, Lord!
I come to do your will.
You do not ask for sacrifice and offerings,
but an open ear.
You do not ask for holocaust and victim.
Instead, here am I.

(From Psalm 40)

Activities
On the activity sheet they are helped to see different ways God calls people, and to explore some of the reasons for listening or refusing to listen. They look at vocation in its broadest sense, both as long-term work and for particular tasks.

Discussion starters
1. Are there occasions when we sense God's call and direction but fail to run with it in case we are mistaken?

2. What makes people able to respond to God's call and what (and who) hinders them?

Notes

GOD CALLS HIS PEOPLE ...

THROUGH PRAYER

THROUGH WHAT THEY READ IN THE BIBLE

THROUGH EVENTS

THROUGH SHARED WORSHIP

WHEN WE'RE ON OUR OWN, BEING QUIET

VOCATION

HOW DO I KNOW IF GOD IS CALLING ME? I DON'T WANT TO MISS IT.

In that case you'll know, because you're expecting to hear from him. But there are ways to check.

LIKE WHAT?

Like—does this call match up with the God I know? Does it seem personally meant for me?

IF IT FEELS RIGHT, WHAT SHOULD I DO?

Tell God you are listening and are ready to go where he leads you. Don't go ahead of God, making things happen. Let him lead you.

WHY LISTEN?

WHY REFUSE TO LISTEN?

Here I am, Lord!
I come to do your will.
You do not ask for sacrifice and offerings,
but an open ear.
You do not ask for holocaust and victim.
Instead, here am I.
(from Psalm 39)

VOCATION (LIKE 'VOCAL') MEANS A CALLING

IT MAY BE A CALLING TO LIFE-LONG WORK

IT MAY BE TO A WAY OF LIFE

IT MAY BE A CALL TO PRAY FOR A PARTICULAR PERSON

YOU MAY BE CALLED TO GET IN TOUCH WITH SOMEONE STRAIGHT AWAY

IT MAY BE FOR A SHORT-TERM PARTICULAR JOB

KEEP YOUR EARS OPEN!

Third Sunday in Ordinary Time

Thought for the day

When we are called we need to respond with obedience so that many may be brought to repentance.

Readings

Jonah 3:1–5, 10
1 Corinthians 7:29–31
Mark 1:14–20

Aim: To look at the call to help people come to repentance.

Starter

Try line dancing, where you are all changing direction as you do the set steps.

Teaching

Read the passage from Jonah, reminding them of what had happened the first time God wanted Jonah to call the citizens of Nineveh to repentance. In today's passage we find Jonah being obedient to his call, and the people also obedient to their calling. They decide to reject their evil ways and turn back to God. God knew that Jonah was the right person for the job, but he could only use him if Jonah willingly agreed. All kinds of good doesn't get done because the people God wants to call aren't listening.

Now read today's gospel. We find Jesus starting out on his ministry, and his message is summed up by Mark as this: "Repent and believe the good news." The reason he needs to call the disciples is so that they can spread that same message far and wide. That way, the call to repent has reached millions of people in every generation since Jesus walked on the beach by the lake!

Talk over together what repentance means. It is a "turning around" to face the right way—to face God rather than living with our backs to him. The reason God is so concerned that people hear the call to repent is because God knows that our only hope for lasting joy and fulfillment is to face this way. The last thing God wants is for people to miss out on the full and lasting life we are designed for.

Praying

Lord, make me know your ways.
Lord, teach me your paths.
Make me walk in your truth, and teach me:
for you are God my Savior.
Amen.

(From Psalm 25)

Activities

The meaning of repentance is reinforced on the worksheet, and they are encouraged to look at how we can call one another to repentance in a loving, positive way. They also have a factfile for Jonah to fill in.

Discussion starters

1. How can we live in the world without being drawn into its dealings at the expense of our spiritual development?

2. Why is it so important to repent? What does repenting involve?

Notes

REPENTANCE

WHAT DOES IT ACTUALLY MEAN TO REPENT?

It means to turn right round and face the right way.

SO YOU'RE TURNING YOUR BACK ON WHAT'S WRONG AND EVIL?

Yes. God is always calling his people to repentance—he knows that we can be happiest and most fulfilled when we're facing the right way.

DO YOU JUST REPENT ONCE OR LOTS OF TIMES?

There's often one time when we really commit ourselves to the right direction, but we all seem to keep turning back to what is selfish, so we have to get into the habit of repenting whenever we need to.

NAME: JONAH

FIRST CALLING: TO TELL PEOPLE AT _____ TO REPENT.

REACTION TO CALLING:

RESULT OF DISOBEDIENCE:

SECOND CALLING:

REACTION TO CALLING:

RESULT OF OBEDIENCE:

TAKE ONE

TAKE TWO

HOW CAN WE HELP ONE ANOTHER ALONG?

One of your group of friends has started taking drugs, and you know she's stealing from her mom's purse. WHAT CAN YOU DO TO HELP HER?

Two of your friends are always arguing and trying to prove which one's better. HOW CAN YOU HELP?

You're going to spend a weekend with a relative you can't stand, and you're worried that you'll lose your temper. HOW CAN YOUR FRIENDS AND FAMILY HELP YOU?

An elderly neighbor is always moaning about the noise of your music. You get woken up by her loud television at 6 am. HOW CAN YOU HELP EACH OTHER?

LORD, MAKE ME KNOW YOUR WAYS. LORD, TEACH ME YOUR PATHS. MAKE ME WALK IN YOUR TRUTH AND TEACH ME: FOR YOU ARE GOD MY SAVIOUR. — AMEN — (— FROM PSALM 24 —)

Fourth Sunday in Ordinary Time

Thought for the day
Jesus displays all the signs that mark him as God's chosen One.

Readings
Deuteronomy 18:15–20
1 Corinthians 7:32–35
Mark 1:21–28

Aim: To trace the prophecies through to the person of Jesus, displaying God's nature in his words and behavior.

Starter
Play a card game in which you try to cheat, but if challenged you have to show whether you have been honest or not. One possibility is this. Deal out the cards equally. Players hide their hand of cards from everyone. Take turns placing cards face down in order of number, saying aloud what you are claiming it to be. If challenged, you must turn the card up, and if you are found to have cheated, you have to take all the cards laid on the table. First to be rid of all their cards wins.

Teaching
One of the top qualities of God is his complete integrity and honesty. God never pretends to us or cheats; his nature is full of truth. As people we often cheat, not just playfully in games but in our lives. We are quite good at doing wrong and pretending to ourselves that it is someone else's fault. If we don't like to think of ourselves as unkind, we'll sometimes pretend that we haven't been unkind, even though we secretly know we have.

That's why it has always been a bit unnerving when people have found God looking into their hearts, and realized that he sees what is really there, and not what we'd like him to find. His light shows up evil and wrong thinking as well as all the good stuff. Read the passage from Deuteronomy 18, noticing how the people even then were rather scared of close contact with the all-seeing God. Then go on to today's gospel. In Jesus, God has come closer to his people than ever before, and there is a man in the congregation who finds this very distressing. Talk over why this might be, in view of what you read in the first reading.

Go back to the Deuteronomy passage and look at the verses about the prophet speaking God's word. Link this with Mark 1:22, so that they can pick up on the authority of Jesus as God's spokesman. Jesus is God's chosen One, and as he expresses God's thoughts and nature, people are bound to notice God's glory shining in him.

Praying
Lord Jesus, as we read about you in the gospels
we can see that you are the Christ,
God's anointed, chosen Savior.
We ask you to shine in us,
so that we are lit up by your truth and love.

Activities
On the activity sheet there is a role-play to try, and an identity markings activity that enables them to consider identity markings of the Messiah.

Discussion starters
1. What signs of glory showed in Jesus?

2. How can we get the right balance between awesome reverence which verges on fear, and familiarity which borders on presumption?

Notes

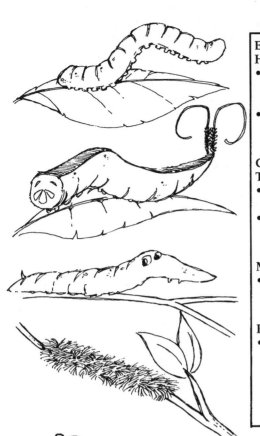

Elephant Hawk Moth
- 2 large eye spots behind the head
- front looks a bit like an elephant's trunk

Garden Tiger Moth
- covered with fuzzy hairs
- often known as a 'woolly bear'

Magpie Moth
- moves in a looping way, arching its back

Puss Moth
- uses its face mask and tail whips to display threateningly to its predators

'I KNOW WHO YOU ARE!'

THAT MAN SOUNDS REALLY FRIGHTENING, SCREAMING AT JESUS LIKE HE HATES HIM.

Yes, I expect it was quite scary to be there.

WHY DID HE THINK JESUS WAS GOING TO DESTROY HIM?

The evil spirit in him knew he was in the presence of God—enough to make any evil spirit panic.

JESUS SEEMS QUITE IN CONTROL, THOUGH.

That's because God's power of good is always stronger than the power of evil, and Jesus just wants to set the man free.

CAN YOU IDENTIFY THESE CATERPILLARS?

WHAT IS IT THAT MARKS JESUS OUT AND IDENTIFIES HIM AS GOD'S CHOSEN ONE?

Peter, one of Jesus' followers, who was there in the synagogue (and had once said to Jesus, 'Go away from me, I'm a sinful man.')

Zeke, the man with an evil spirit, who has been sorted out by Jesus this morning

A visitor to Capernaum who hasn't heard what happened

YOU ALL MEET UP ON THE SABBATH, AFTER GOING TO THE SYNAGOGUE IN CAPERNAUM.

Rebecca, who heard Jesus teaching before the healing, and was very impressed with his authority

LORD JESUS, AS WE READ ABOUT YOU IN THE GOSPELS WE CAN SEE THAT YOU ARE THE CHRIST, GOD'S ANOINTED, CHOSEN SAVIOUR. WE ASK YOU TO SHINE IN US, SO THAT WE ARE LIT UP BY YOUR TRUTH AND LOVE.

Fifth Sunday in Ordinary Time

Thought for the day
The good news about God is far too good to keep to ourselves.

Readings
Job 7:1–4, 6–7
1 Corinthians 9:16–19, 22–23
Mark 1:29–39

Aim: To focus on what the good news is and how we can spread it.

Starter
Have a selection of newspaper headlines and stories. These are to be sorted into different categories:

- Gossip
- The odd/unusual
- Important good news
- Important bad news

Teaching
Leading on from the starter, talk together about what we consider is news worth spreading around in our newspapers each day. Notice which kinds of stories are considered most newsworthy, and whether good news is considered worth printing. If they were to become an editor, would they want to change what is thought of as worth spreading?

Now read today's gospel, looking at why Jesus wants to move on from Capernaum. What is it that he has seen in the eyes of those he has healed which makes him anxious to spread the good news as widely as possible? (Such things as joy and freedom from pain or guilt; they look as if they have just been set free.) The news we have to tell about Jesus is worth telling because lives can be set free as a result of knowing it. People surely have a right to know something that has the power to change their lives for the better.

Read the passage from 1 Corinthians to see how, for Paul, too, telling people about God's real power and presence is an urgent matter—he can't bear for anyone to be left without the opportunity to know God and benefit from his saving love.

Praying
O God,
let no one miss out on knowing you
because I failed to let them know about you.
But rather let many be brought to love you
because of my words and actions.

Activities
On the activity sheet they are encouraged to think through the value of telling people certain information, both good and bad, and the responsibility of those who are in the know to inform other people of risks and benefits. They can then discuss what they want people to know about God, and how this might best be communicated to those who don't know God at all.

Discussion starters
1. What would you most want people to know about God?

2. What do you think is the best way of telling them?

Notes

Sixth Sunday in Ordinary Time

Thought for the day

Jesus wants to heal us to wholeness, and to him no one is untouchable.

Readings

Leviticus 13:1–2, 44–46
1 Corinthians 10:31—11:1
Mark 1:40–45

Aim: To see how God feels about untouchables.

Starter

On separate pieces of cardboard, write out the following: a tramp; a mother with a noisy baby; a white man; a black man; a person with flu; a person with leprosy; a tattooed skinhead; a pretty girl; a handsome young man; an old lady who smells; a smoker; a disabled person; someone from a rival school.

Spread these cards out and let the group suggest a rating of 1–10 for their response to this question in each case: "Would you be happy sitting on a crowded bus next to …?"

Teaching

In the previous activity we could see that most of us have hang-ups about close contact with people in certain situations, for all kinds of reasons. It's easy to see why society clubs together to isolate certain groups, treating them as outsiders. Our readings today help us to see what God's attitude is to social outcasts and "untouchables."

Begin by reading the gospel from Mark 1. Point out that in law this man was ritually unclean, and anyone touching him would be considered contaminated, and therefore unclean themselves. What was Jesus showing by touching the leper as part of the healing? Was it just the leprosy he was healing, or would the man have also been emotionally healed in some way by the touch?

Jesus' great desire to help the man to wholeness obviously overcame any thoughts of contamination; he reckoned it worth being "contaminated," worth being thought "unclean." How does that link up with the idea of the Incarnation—"Word of the Father, now in flesh appearing"? What does it all tell us about God and his attitude to us?

Now look at the passage from Corinthians, where Paul advises us all to check our own behavior seriously. In view of today's gospel, how do we measure up? Do we reach out to touch, or do we go along with what everyone else considers OK to ignore and avoid?

Praying

Lord God, make me willing
to reach out with your love
and touch the lives
and look into the eyes
of those whom the world despises and avoids.
Amen.

Activities

On the activity sheet there are examples of people working with the rejected and considering it a privilege as well as a responsibility. You could add to these with other examples, or invite someone in the parish who is working in such an area to join the group. There is also a thinking exercise to face the uncomfortable "reasons" we have for rejecting and marginalizing people. This week's teaching could well lead the group on to think of ways they can get more actively involved with local projects.

Discussion starters

1. Are there habits of social behavior we have become so used to that we fail to see in them the marginalization and degrading that is going on?

2. Do we ignore injustice when to act or speak out might make us unpopular? As Christians, what can we do about this?

Notes

IF YOU WANT TO, YOU CAN ooo

SO THE LEPER BELIEVED THAT JESUS WAS ABLE TO CURE HIM?

Yes, he believed in Jesus' power, but he wasn't sure Jesus would want to do it.

THAT WAS A BIT OF AN INSULT, WASN'T IT? I MEAN, OF COURSE JESUS WOULD WANT TO HEAL HIM!

Exactly. But Jesus picks up on the way the man seems to think he's rubbish, and shows him that he isn't.

HOW?

By touching him! (He's supposed to be untouchable, remember.) And the man is healed.

YES, IT'S THE CALCUTTA HOME FOR THE DESTITUTE AND DYING, BUT IT'S A HAPPY PLACE, FULL OF PEACE AND QUIET JOY. IT'S A GREAT PRIVILEGE TO BE HERE!

WE PROVIDE A HOT MEAL AND SHELTER FOR THE NIGHT.

IT'S NOT MUCH, BUT IT'S THE LEAST WE CAN DO, ISN'T IT?

WHAT DO YOU THINK MAKES SOMEONE THINK OF ANOTHER HUMAN BEING AS UNTOUCHABLE?

LORD GOD, MAKE ME WILLING TO REACH OUT WITH YOUR LOVE AND TOUCH THE LIVES OF THOSE WHOM THE WORLD DESPISES AND AVOIDS.
– AMEN –

They are 'different'	
They are offensive to look at	
They are offensive to listen to	
They are too poor	
They are too rich	
They threaten your own health	
They are embarrassing	
They are too demanding	

BUT ARE THESE **VALID** REASONS???

Seventh Sunday in Ordinary Time

Thought for the day

The Son of Man has authority on earth to forgive sins.

Readings

Isaiah 43:18–19, 21–22, 24–25
2 Corinthians 1:18–22
Mark 2:1–12

Aim: To explore the nature of God's forgiveness and Jesus' claims of identity.

Starter

Who am I? They have twenty questions in which to discover the identity of a chosen character. All questions can only be answered with a "Yes" or "No."

Teaching

First read the gospel together, with different people taking the parts and everyone reading the crowd's words. Look at what the scribes are thinking and wondering about. Why do they say, "Only God can forgive sins"? Refer to the passage from Isaiah 43, seeing what God, through the prophet, has to say. Draw out that it is all part of God's loving goodness to forgive sins—his very nature is to do it. Look at what forgiveness actually means, using the sheet to focus your ideas, and then refer to 2 Corinthians 1:18–21. What does the gospel show in verses 19 and 20? In Jesus forgiving the man's sins and healing him, he is acting out God's nature. So did he have the authority to forgive sins? Yes, because he was showing that he must indeed be the Son of God.

Praying

I'm accepted, I'm forgiven,
I am fathered by the true and living God.
I'm accepted, no condemnation,
I am loved by the true and living God.
There's no guilt or fear as I draw near
to the Savior and Creator of the world.
There is joy and peace as I release
my worship to you, O Lord.

(Rob Hayward
© 1985 Kingsway's Thankyou Music/EMI Christian Music Publishing)

Activities

On the activity sheet they are encouraged to look at what forgiveness is, when we need it and how it can change our lives. It is important that they realize Christians are not perfect just because they go to church, and the church is full of redeemed sinners. They also need to know that the forgiveness is not a one-time event, after which we lose the chance of God forgiving us again. There is *always* the opportunity to confess our sin to God and know his healing forgiveness.

Discussion starters

1. How can forgiveness be a healing?

2. In what way is Christ the eternal "Yes"?

Notes

66

Eighth Sunday in Ordinary Time

Thought for the day

The long-expected bridegroom is Christ, and the church is his bride. We cannot half-attend the wedding feast, but must wholeheartedly join in the celebrations.

Readings

Hosea 2:16–17, 21–22
2 Corinthians 3:1–6
Mark 2:18–22

Aim: To explore the bridegroom imagery, and look at the importance of having new wineskins for the new wine of God's kingdom.

Starter

Have a few atlases and some wine bottles or labels. They are going to discover where each wine comes from.

Teaching

Look at some of the information on a wine label. We know where it comes from and how old it is, as well as what it tastes like and whether it will last. Explain how new wine is still very lively, and in Jesus' time it was important to put it in strong new skins, as otherwise it would burst the skins. One of the times when wine is often drunk is at weddings, and our readings today describe God's relationship with his people as rather like a bridegroom faithfully committing himself to his bride.

Read the passage from Hosea and pick up on the love and commitment of God to his people. Psalm 103 also celebrates the enormous forgiving love God has for us.

When Jesus came it was like the bridegroom coming in person, so that the wedding festivities could really begin. People did notice that Jesus wasn't leading his disciples in times of great fasting, like John the Baptist and the Pharisees, and they felt that as a holy man he ought to be fasting, rather than feasting. Read today's gospel up to verse 20 to see how Jesus answers their criticism.

When did Jesus mean that his disciples would be fasting? After the crucifixion? What about once the Holy Spirit had filled them at Pentecost? What about now? In one way we have the bridegroom with us, and celebrate his real presence in the bread and wine at every Eucharist. At the same time we are looking forward to when Jesus returns in glory, so we are both with the bridegroom and waiting for him. This is reflected in our times of celebration and our times of fasting.

Now look at the second part of the gospel. What is Jesus talking about? Patching old clothes with new unshrunk material certainly doesn't work, any more than putting new wine in old wineskins. But what is Jesus really talking about here? Remind them of God's total love and faithful commitment to his people. The new wine of the kingdom of God is the new risen life we are offered through Jesus saving us from sin and death. To have this in us we need to be remade as containers so that we can safely contain it.

Praying

Spirit of the living God, fall afresh on me!
Spirit of the living God, fall afresh on me!
Melt me, mold me, fill me, use me,
Spirit of the living God, fall afresh on me.

(Daniel Iverson
© 1963 Birdwing Music/EMI Christian Music Publishing)

Activities

On the activity sheet they look at the passage from 2 Corinthians, and how committed, renewed Christian people can be living letters of recommendation. They also look at how Christian lives shabbily lived can direct others away from God. They look at what real commitment is all about.

Discussion starters

1. Do we try to sew on the odd patch of God's new life to our familiar and comfortable cloaks of the old life, rather than accepting the completely new wedding garment which Jesus offers us?

2. Are we taking seriously the need to nurture new Christians, or do we concentrate on pouring in new wine without addressing the state of the wineskins?

Notes

Ninth Sunday in Ordinary Time

Thought for the day
Jesus has the words of eternal life—he sheds light on a right attitude to the Law.

Readings
Deuteronomy 5:12–15
2 Corinthians 4:6–11
Mark 2:23—3:6

Aim: To explore the nature of the Law and Jesus' interpretation of it.

Starter
Play dodgeball. Have one person stand in the center with the others in a circle, passing the ball and throwing it to aim at the person's legs. Whoever hits the person in the middle then takes a turn themselves to be in the middle.

Teaching
First read the passage from Deuteronomy 5, and have a brief look at the ten commandments, which are on the sheet. The spirit of the whole Law is love for God and love for neighbor, and in an effort to protect them and uphold them well, the teachers of the Law had got hung up on all the details and had lost sight of the real spirit of the Law.

Now go on to read today's gospel, looking out for the way Jesus is going to deal with this over-zealous keeping of the letter of the Law, while shutting out the loving spirit of it. At what level are the teachers correct about Jesus breaking the Law, and at what level are they mistaken? Notice how Jesus doesn't draw away from doing what is right, even when it makes him dangerously unpopular with the authorities; never does he compromise God's values in order to protect his position.

Finally, look at 2 Corinthians 4:6–11. In a way it interprets Jesus' actions in the gospel, showing how he shines God's light in our hearts so that we can understand God better. That is bound to affect the way we live. It should prevent us getting so set in our ways and traditions that we stop bothering to listen to God's directing; it should give us an ideal by which to measure our attitudes to those in need.

Praying
Lord God, teach us your ways
of compassion and mercy,
so that the way we treat others
may be in line with the way you treat us.
Amen.

Activities
On the activity sheet there are the ten commandments and Jesus' summary of the Law, to use as a daily guide for right attitudes and behavior. There is also space to put down all the present involvement of the parish with caring outreach. Any gaps can be noted and prayed about regularly, with ideas for action taken seriously.

Discussion starters
1. "Love God and do what you like." Is this famous remark of St. Augustine a helpful way of looking at the commandments, or should we be taking the actual laws more seriously than we do?

2. What do you think might horrify Jesus today, and might need his teaching?

Notes

1. You shall have no other gods besides me.

2. Don't take God's name and use it as a swear word.

3. Keep the Sabbath day holy and as a day of rest.

4. Honor your father and mother.

5. You shall not murder.

6. You shall not commit adultery.

7. You shall not steal.

8. You shall not give false witness against your neighbor.

9. You shall not long for others' partners.

10. You shall not long for others' possessions.

THE TEN COMMANDMENTS

ALL OF WHICH CAN BE SUMMARISED AS:

LOVE GOD AND LOVE ONE ANOTHER

... ARE WE ?

WHAT GOD'S LAW IS ALL ABOUT

HOW COULD THE TEACHERS OF THE LAW THINK IT WAS WRONG FOR JESUS TO HEAL THE MAN ?

Look at commandment No. 4.

BUT JESUS WAS DOING GOOD AND SETTING THE MAN FREE.

Exactly. He wanted to show the teachers that the Law is to help us, but not imprison us.

I THINK IT'S JUST AS HARD TO LOVE GOD AND ONE ANOTHER.

Yes, if we really lived by those rules, what other rules would we need?

MAKE A NOTE OF ALL THE CARING OUTREACH IN YOUR CHURCH.

MAKE A NOTE OF THE NEEDS OF THE COMMUNITY.

WHAT ARE THE GAPS ?

WHAT NEEDS ARE THERE IN YOUR AREA ?

LORD GOD, TEACH US YOUR WAYS OF COMPASSION AND MERCY, SO THAT THE WAY WE TREAT OTHERS MAY BE IN LINE WITH THE WAY YOU TREAT US.
—AMEN—

Tenth Sunday in Ordinary Time

Thought for the day
Anyone who does God's will is considered a close family member of Jesus.

Readings
Genesis 3:9–15
2 Corinthians 4:13—5:1
Mark 3:20–35

Aim: To look at the scribes' accusations and Jesus' response.

Starter
Play basketball using a Nerf ball or a beach ball, and a bucket or bin for the net. Play first with even sides, and then with everyone on the same side, and no opponents. Compare the scores!

Teaching
It is so much easier to score goals when we don't have any opposition! Today we are going to look at some opposition Jesus was faced with, and how he dealt with it.

It wasn't just when Jesus was around that people went against God's way of love. Read the passage from Genesis to see that, right from the beginning, people have been self-willed, and their sin creates a rift between themselves and God; they no longer feel comfortable in his company. That is just as true now; we only feel comfortable in God's company when we are choosing to face his way and are being honest with him. Otherwise we try to hide from him, and avoid his company.

Now read today's gospel, looking out for any friction and opposition to his work. There are two main areas in this reading—the accusation of the scribes, and the concerned family, coming to "take charge" of Jesus.

What do the scribes accuse Jesus of doing? (Casting out demons by the power of demons.) Would this make logical sense? How does Jesus respond to what they are saying about him? (If Satan was fighting against himself in that way, his power would crash.) Logic proves that Jesus cannot be in league with Satan if he is overcoming evil spirits in people.

What about his family—why have they come, and why doesn't Jesus rush off home with them as they would like? Having heard the reports of the crowds surrounding Jesus all the time, giving him no time even to eat, and all the casting-out of evil spirits, they are anxious for him and don't understand that his work on earth is very important, and needs to be done, even if it's sometimes dangerous. He can't spend his life living quietly at home with his immediate family, or the saving work would not get done.

Sometimes families have to share their loved ones with a wider circle of people, and Jesus wants to include as close family all those who are doing their best to live God's way. That is the "family likeness" which marks many people out to be members of Jesus' family.

Praying
Make me a channel of your peace.
Where there is hatred, let me bring your love.
Where there is injury, your pardon, Lord,
and where there's doubt, true faith in you.

(Taken from the song by Sebastian Temple,
based on the Prayer of St. Francis
© 1967 OCP Publications, Portland, OR, USA)

Activities
On the activity sheet there is space to put in an imagined subscript of Jesus' family, in order to put Jesus' reply in context. They can also draw a cartoon to get at the meaning of the scribes' accusations and Jesus' response. Some comments by those struggling with family expectations and God's calling can be used as discussion starters.

Discussion starters
1. It is quite an honor to be considered Jesus' close relatives! Do we behave as if this is true? Do we show any family likenesses?

2. What does it mean in practical terms to pray to God our Father: "Let your will be done on earth as it is done in heaven"?

Notes

HE IS OUT OF HIS MIND.

WE ARE GOING TO TAKE CHARGE OF HIM.

WHEN THEY SAID THIS ... WHAT WERE THEY THINKING?

WE'VE HEARD THAT ...

WE WILL ...

WE'RE WORRIED THAT ...

THE OPPOSITION

WHAT WERE THE SCRIBES SAYING ABOUT JESUS?

That he could only drive out demons from people because he was in league with Satan.

SO THEY WERE SAYING HIS POWER WASN'T GOOD BUT EVIL?

That's right.

BUT THAT WOULD BE LIKE SCORING AN OWN GOAL!

Exactly. Jesus pointed that out – if Satan was working against himself like that he would collapse.

HOW WAS JESUS REALLY ABLE TO DRIVE OUT DEMONS?

With God's power of total goodness and love. Evil is no match for that.

FAMILY MATTERS

MARK 3:20-35

At first I was upset when Judith said she was going to work in Africa. I mean, I needed her to pop in and see me, and she's my daughter. But when I saw what God was doing through her there, I could see I had to let her go. And God has given me some wonderful friends at church who pop in.

I knew God was calling me to be a missionary doctor, and I'm needed here. But it meant I had to leave my mother on her own for three years. That was hard for us.

SOMETIMES THERE'S A CONFLICT OF INTERESTS...

MAKE ME A CHANNEL OF YOUR PEACE. WHERE THERE IS HATRED, LET ME BRING YOUR LOVE. WHERE THERE IS INJURY, YOUR PARDON, LORD, AND WHERE THERE'S DOUBT, TRUE FAITH IN YOU.

(From the song by Sebastian Temple, based on the Prayer of St Francis, © 1967 OCP Publications, USA)

CARTOON TIME – MARK 3:27

Eleventh Sunday in Ordinary Time

Thought for the day

From small beginnings, and by God's power, the kingdom of heaven grows.

Readings

Ezekiel 17:22–24
2 Corinthians 5:6–10
Mark 4:26–34

Aim: To look at Jesus' teaching on the growth of the kingdom of heaven.

Starter

If you have one of those Christmas angels with lit candles that move around and around, set it up and let the children watch it while they try to figure out what keeps the movement going. Other appropriate "machines" would be lava lamps, or kites.

Teaching

First have a look at the Old Testament passage from Ezekiel. Explain first that King Nebuchadnezzar had taken the important people of Israel off into Babylon, and the prophet had described this as a great eagle tearing off the top branches of a cedar tree and planting it in a land of traders. Now, in contrast to the worldly way of doing things, we look at God's way of renewing and redeeming a hopeless situation.

Bring out the point that God decides what he will do and does it for greatest good. We are called to work with him, rather than just follow our own whims and fancies; the important thing is to check constantly with God what his will actually is. That way we will be less likely to find ourselves working in opposition to God.

Now read Mark 4:26–34. Look out for where the growing power lies. (Farmers and gardeners don't create the growth themselves, but work with the creative God to allow God's natural growing power to happen.) If we do our best to provide the best conditions for people's faith to grow, the actual growth of the kingdom is going to happen through the loving God's power and will.

Finally look at this week's section of 2 Corinthians. Whether we are in this life or the next, our only goal is to please God. It is the love of Christ in us that controls us, enabling us to live fruitfully—his freely given gift rather than our hard work.

Praying

It is a good thing to give thanks to the Lord,
and to sing praises to your name, O Most High;
to tell of your loving kindness early in the morning
and of your faithfulness in the night season.

(From Psalm 92)

Activities

There is a short sketch on the activity sheet about a sunbathing farmer who is busy growing his crop, and they are encouraged to explore the quiet, hidden growing of the kingdom of God. There is also a checklist for looking at signs of spiritual growing, both as individuals and in their church community.

Discussion starters

1. Do we sometimes block God's growing kingdom by wanting it to happen in a particular way for us, our family, or our church?

2. Is it possible to work too hard for the coming of the kingdom?

Notes

- Excuse me, but shouldn't you be working? I mean . . . you're a farmer, aren't you?

- Uh? . . . Oh . . . working! Should I be working? What do you mean – I AM working!

- But here you are, sunbathing! How can that be work?

- Well, I assure you I'm working very hard! I'm growing oats, wheat and barley at the moment.

- Oh, yeah? Then they can't be growing very well if you're here snoozing, can they?

- Ah, well, that's just where you're wrong! I planted those seeds, right? And now they're growing – whether I'm watching them at it or not! You just come back in a month and see for yourself!

SO ... HOW DOES THE KINGDOM GROW?

IT IS A GOOD THING TO GIVE
THANKS TO THE LORD,
AND TO SING PRAISES TO
YOUR NAME, O MOST HIGH;
TO TELL OF YOUR LOVING
KINDNESS EARLY IN THE MORNING
AND OF YOUR FAITHFULNESS
IN THE NIGHT SEASON.
(– FROM PSALM 91 –)

GOD'S KINGDOM GROWS

IS JESUS SAYING WE DON'T NEED TO DO ANYTHING TO HELP THE KINGDOM GROW?

No, but he's reminding us that the actual growing is God's business, and it happens.

SO IS OUR JOB TO GET THE GROUND READY AND KEEP IT FREE OF RUBBLE AND WEEDS?

Yes! We work with God on that, and planting the seed. Then God can bring those seeds to harvest.

I SUPPOSE IT'S A BIT POMPOUS TO THINK IT'S ALL DOWN TO OUR HARD WORK.

Yes – a bit like a driver thinking he makes a car go along.

SIGNS OF KINGDOM GROWTH?

I think the signs to look for would be ...

1	2
3	4

Can you see them?

Here	1	2	3	4
In yourself				
In your church community				
In our society				

Twelfth Sunday
in Ordinary Time

Thought for the day

What kind of person is this? Even the wind and waves obey him.

Readings

Job 38:1, 8–11
2 Corinthians 5:14–17
Mark 4:35–41

Aim: To explore the implications of the calming of the storm.

Starter

What are we? Explain that they are some kind of group with some kind of leader, and they can work out what they are by asking the leader questions (yes/no answers only). They may be objects, animals or people, or a combination. To start them off they are given one clue.

Here are some possible scenarios:

- A group of planes at different flying levels, waiting to be given permission to land from ground control. (Clue: airline peanuts, airline pillow, and an emergency chart)

- Swallows perched on a telegraph wire gathering in the autumn for their leader to set them off on migration to Africa. (Clue: a feather)

- A mountain rescue team in thick fog, guided by the compass. (Clue: A map and a first aid kit)

Teaching

What does it mean for God to be in charge? First read the chosen Old Testament passage, looking at it from this point of view. Notice what it does and doesn't mean—responsible loving, picking up pieces, drawing together and planning, yet following natural laws and allowing us the freedom of choice.

Now read from Mark's gospel the account of Jesus calming the wind and waves.

Why do they think the disciples woke Jesus up?

Do they think they would all have drowned if Jesus hadn't commanded the weather to calm down?

Why might Jesus have chosen to do this instead of comforting the disciples and cheering them through the difficult situation? (Feeling compassion for them/showing a sign?/fighting with evil?)

What did it help the disciples to understand about Jesus in a very dramatic lesson?

What does it help us to see about Jesus as we read the account nearly two thousand years later?

Share ideas and other questions they may have.

Praying

Lead us, heavenly Father, lead us
o'er the world's tempestuous sea.
Guard us, guide us, keep us, feed us,
for we have no help but thee.
Yet possessing every blessing
if our God our Father be.

Activities

On the activity sheet there are some of the questions people ask about God intervening, and hints and references are given to help them work out possible answers. They are also invited to look at possible storms into which Jesus speaks calmly—in their own lives, in the church and in the news. This can all lead to prayer and action.

Discussion starters

1. When were you last stunned by the awesome power of the living God? Share your experiences and how they affected your understanding of God.

2. If people know something of what God is really like, how is it likely to affect the way they pray?

Notes

Thirteenth Sunday in Ordinary Time

Thought for the day
God's power can reach even into death and draw out life.

Readings
Wisdom 1:13–15; 2:23–24
2 Corinthians 8:7, 9, 13–15
Mark 5:21–43

Aim: To explore the implications of this healing from death.

Starter
Use a stop watch and have someone begin talking for one minute on a particular subject. They can be interrupted and challenged for repetitions or hesitations, after which the challenger continues the talk. Whoever is talking when the stop watch goes off is the winner.

Teaching
Talk a little together about how sad it is when someone we know and love dies, and how we miss seeing them.

Now make a point of moving to the New Testament, and find Mark's gospel. Read this with different voices taking the various parts. Are they surprised at Jesus actually raising the dead? What does this show his followers? Why do they think only a few were allowed to be present?

Also look at the healing which takes place on the way to Jairus' house. How do they think Jairus might have been feeling while Jesus took time to talk to the woman? How do they cope with urgent interruptions? What if the interruption was the reason the little girl was already dead—might this be why Jesus was prepared to bring her back from the dead?

Finally look at what Mark shows us about faith. Where do faith and believing come up in the two healings of today's gospel? What does Jesus say about it?

Praying
Be still, for the power of the Lord
is moving in this place;
he comes to cleanse and heal, to minister his grace.
No work too hard for him,
in faith receive from him.
Be still, for the power of the Lord
is moving in this place.

(Taken from the song *Be still, for the presence* by David J. Evans © 1986 Kingsway's Thankyou Music/EMI Christian Music Publishing)

Activities
There is a role-play on the activity sheet to help them see today's gospel from various different standpoints, and there is space for them to record what this account reveals of the nature of Jesus and his mission.

Discussion starters
1. The situation in the gospel of urgent business being interrupted by another crisis is all too familiar! What can we learn from Jesus' way of dealing with it?
2. Paul talks of us giving generously within our means (2 Corinthians). What does this mean in terms not just of money but time, commitment and even faith and trust?

Notes

HE IS HERE TO SHOW US HOW POWERFUL GOD'S LOVE IS

SO WHAT DOES THIS REVEAL ABOUT JESUS AND HIS MISSION?

HE MUST BE GOD'S SON

HE SPEAKS WITH AUTHORITY BIGGER THAN DEATH

TO TEACH HIS DISCIPLES WHO HE IS

HE FEELS SORRY FOR PEOPLE WHO ARE SAD

HE HAS COME TO BRING US ALL TO LIFE

JESUS

HIS MISSION

RAISING THE DEAD

IS JAIRUS' DAUGHTER THE ONLY PERSON JESUS RAISED FROM THE DEAD?

No – Jesus brought a young man to life because he felt sorry for the widowed mother. And when Lazarus, Jesus' friend, had died, Jesus raised him after he'd been dead for four days.

IT JUST SEEMS SO IMPOSSIBLE TO BRING ANYONE TO LIFE AGAIN – UNLESS THEY WEREN'T COMPLETELY DEAD YET.

Well, don't forget we're looking at the Lord of life here – not just anybody. Actually Jesus tells the girl's parents that she is only sleeping but they just laugh at him.

THE GIRL WAS MADE COMPLETELY BETTER, WASN'T SHE?

Oh yes – and she was very hungry!

BECKY
* JAIRUS' 12 - YEAR - OLD DAUGHTER
* DANGEROUSLY ILL
* JESUS BROUGHT HER BACK TO LIFE

JAIRUS
* WORRIED AND SAD
* HAS FAITH THAT JESUS CAN HELP
* LOVES HIS YOUNG DAUGHTER
* CONVINCED SHE IS REALLY DEAD

JAMES, JOHN AND PETER
* THE 3 DISCIPLES ALLOWED TO WATCH
* WITH JESUS EVERY DAY
* WONDERING WHO JESUS CAN BE

BE STILL, FOR THE POWER OF THE LORD IS MOVING IN THIS PLACE;
HE COMES TO CLEANSE AND HEAL,
TO MINISTER HIS GRACE.
NO WORK TOO HARD FOR HIM,
IN FAITH RECEIVE FROM HIM.
BE STILL, FOR THE POWER OF THE LORD IS MOVING IN THIS PLACE.

(Taken from the song *Be Still, For the Presence* by David J. Evans, © 1986 Kingsway's Thankyou Music/EMI Christian Music Publishing)

1. READ THE ACCOUNT IN MARK 5
2. TAKE ON ONE OF THE ROLES
3. EACH CHARACTER TELLS THE STORY FROM THEIR OWN POINT OF VIEW

Fourteenth Sunday in Ordinary Time

Thought for the day
If we are not ready to listen to the truth, we will not hear it.

Readings
Ezekiel 2:2–5
2 Corinthians 12:7–10
Mark 6:1–6

Aim: To look at how the message is to be preached, whether people want to listen or not.

Starter
Play "pick-up-sticks," either with a commercial set, or by tipping a pile of silverware onto the table and taking turns lifting off one item at a time very carefully, so as not to wobble the rest.

Teaching
That was a bit how it feels to be talking about our faith to someone who is determined not to believe a word of what we're saying! We have to go very carefully and sensitively, looking out for where those people are coming from, so we can talk into their questions and help them understand. Today we are reading about the way the people in Jesus' hometown reacted to him. Read Mark 6:1–6 and look for why they rejected him.

Now read the passage from Ezekiel, where the prophet is told to tell God's words, even though he knows there will be many who refuse to listen. Talk together about our own lives and the people we know. How are they to be told about the God who made them and who longs for them to live freely in his forgiving love, instead of living just for material things and personal comfort?

Pray for one another in the group about particular situations that come up in the conversation, and particular people they want to help hear God's message.

Praying
Lord, help me to listen properly
so that I hear your voice, your will for me,
your comfort and your challenges.
And help me to speak out your good news
so others may hear your voice, your will for them,
your comfort and your challenges.
Amen.

Activities
On the activity sheet there is a short script to draw their attention to different ways of not listening, and some help with training ourselves into a habit of daily prayer. They are also encouraged to look at how the call to pass on God's message affects them.

Discussion starters
1. How genuinely receptive are we to God's word? Do we mark out "no-go" areas where God is concerned?
2. How might our gut reactions alert us to God trying to tell us something important, which we don't really want to hear?

Notes

THE BASIC SCRIPT

Can I talk to you for a minute? It's just that . . . well, I've been noticing how you're treating Cliff lately, and it bothers me. You look at him as if he's a slug, and snap his head off whenever you speak.

RESPONSE (A)

Fidget, shuffle, avoid eye contact, look at your watch. Interrupt to say your bus is due.

RESPONSE (B)

Angry, accuse them of always getting at you and always criticizing. Refuse to accept what they say.

RESPONSE (C)

Change the subject and talk over the other person till they give up.

CHOOSE A RESPONSE AND TRY IT OUT WHILE SOMEONE DOES THE BASIC SCRIPT.

THERE ARE LOTS OF WAYS WE MANAGE NOT TO LISTEN!

I DIDN'T WANT TO HEAR THAT!

IT DOESN'T FEEL NICE TO HAVE WRONG THINGS POINTED OUT — EVEN IF YOU KNOW THEY'RE TRUE.

I agree. People have never found prophets easy to listen to.

THEY MUST BE BRAVE TO GO ON SPEAKING OUT GOD'S WORD WHEN IT MAKES THEM UNPOPULAR.

Yes. But God does give us the courage to do it, and the words to say.

I BAPTISE YOU IN THE NAME OF THE FATHER...

AM I CALLED TO FIGHT AGAINST EVIL?

FIGHT VALIANTLY AS A DISCIPLE OF CHRIST AGAINST SIN, THE WORLD AND THE DEVIL!

LORD, HELP ME TO LISTEN PROPERLY SO THAT I HEAR YOUR VOICE, YOUR WILL FOR ME, YOUR COMFORT AND YOUR CHALLENGES. HELP ME TO SPEAK OUT YOUR GOOD NEWS SO OTHERS MAY HEAR YOUR VOICE, YOUR WILL FOR THEM, YOUR COMFORT AND YOUR CHALLENGES.
— AMEN —

SUNDAY	MONDAY	TUESDAY	WEDNESDAY	THURSDAY	FRIDAY	SATURDAY	SUNDAY
Make a regular time for prayer each day	Try lighting a 'prayer candle' as you pray	Use the sections of the Lord's Prayer like headings of prayer	Keep a prayer note book to pray for different people each day of the week	Spread out the newspaper and 'pray' the news	Have photos of those you pray for	Include – Penitence, Praise, Thanks, Intercession, Adoration	Check with yourself each Sunday to keep up the habit

SOME HINTS AND IDEAS ...

GET IN TRAINING GET THE DAILY PRAYER HABIT

Fifteenth Sunday in Ordinary Time

Thought for the day
Those who speak out God's will are bound to be vulnerable to rejection and abuse.

Readings
Amos 7:12–15
Ephesians 1:3–14
Mark 6:7–13

Aim: To look at why speaking out God's truth is often dangerous.

Starter
Tie a length of string across the room at just above head height and provide two different colored balloons. Split the group on either side of the string, each with a balloon. Both sides try to get their balloon to touch the floor on the other side, while preventing the other balloon from coming to land on their own side.

Teaching
Draw attention to the way we all did our best to hit that approaching balloon back where it came from. We do just the same in arguments. If someone says something about us that we don't want to hear, we hit it back as fast as we can. Today we are reading about the way prophets are treated when they go on speaking out God's words which people don't want to hear.

Read the Amos passage, noticing in both how faithfulness to God is despised and rejected. Then read today's gospel, where Jesus tells his disciples that people may not want to listen to them. Suppose instead of shutting their ears to what the disciples had to say, they did listen. What might happen?

When we shut our ears to hearing what God wants us to know, we shut out all kinds of possible good in our lives, and open up all kinds of possibilities of evil.

If you have time, look at Ephesians 1:3–14. It is Christ's life in us, and the forgiveness of our sins that makes it possible for us to live God's way—we can't do it on our own without his grace. Also it's important that they understand God's love for us doesn't depend on how well we behave. Getting our lives upright in God's sight is our response to the love God lavishes on us, not the way to earn his love.

Praying
Refiner's fire,
my heart's one desire is to be holy,
set apart for you, Lord.
I choose to be holy,
set apart for you, my Master,
ready to do your will.

(Taken from the song *Purify my heart* by Brian Doerksen © 1990 Mercy/Vineyard Publishing)

Activities
On the activity sheet there are some quotations from people imprisoned for continuing to live God's way even when it is dangerous, and they are looking at what they can do to support those in prison at the moment for their faith, or other Christians locally who could do with some encouragement.

Discussion starters
1. How ready are we to speak out God's truth and God's values when we know they will make us unpopular?
2. How can we best support and encourage the young people as they live and work in environments often openly hostile to God?

Notes

Sheila Cassidy is a doctor. She was imprisoned and tortured for treating a wounded person whom the ruling party disapproved of. She is a Christian.

"I think it was during this time of waiting that I was conscious of praying. I remember little except that I prayed for strength to withstand the pain and for courage to die with dignity if that was to be my fate. Most of all I remember a curious feeling of sharing in Christ's passion. Sick and numb with pain and fear, spread-eagled so vulnerably on the bunk, it came to me that this was perhaps a little how it had been for him one Friday morning so many years before."

From Audacity to Believe
© 1992 Darton, Longman & Todd Ltd

° SHEILA CASSIDY
° DOCTOR IN CHILE

Michele Guinness is Jewish. She became a Christian and her family at first disowned her.

"My fingers trembled on the dial, then somehow found the right numbers. It was ringing.

Oh, let them be out, please!

'Hello! Oh, it's you, darling. How are things?'

'Mom, I'm going to be baptized.'

The silence seemed interminable.

'I said . . .'

'I know what you said.' The voice was cold and hard. 'Never come home again. You're no longer our daughter.'

Click! The line was dead."

From Child of the Covenant
© 1985 Hodder & Stoughton Ltd

° MICHELE GUINNESS

BEING A CHRISTIAN CAN BE DANGEROUS

HOW CAN IT BE DANGEROUS TO LIVE LOVINGLY AND DO WHAT'S RIGHT? Because you may find people tease you or are nasty to you for doing that, and for going to church and for praying.

SUPPOSE I JUST PRETEND I'M NOT A CHRISTIAN? You can do that. But if, as a Christian, you see things happening which you know are offensive to God, you might feel you have to speak out.

BUT DIDN'T JESUS PROMISE TO GIVE US THE WORDS TO SAY WHEN THAT HAPPENS? Yes! And he will keep that promise. Even if you are insulted, God will keep you and protect you from evil whatever happens.

Gonville f-Beytagh was Dean of the Anglican Cathedral in Johannesburg, South Africa. At that time, concern for black Africans was seen as treason, and he was imprisoned, in solitary confinement.

"To have nothing to do is a devastating, destroying thing; I learned that through being unemployed in the slump in the 1930s when I wasn't wanted by anybody. I learned it too in solitary confinement. On one day I crawled around the floor of my cell and found some bristles from a broom. I spent a long time weaving them into a tiny cross, and that was good because I had found something to do."

From A Glimpse of Glory
© 1986 Paulist Press

° GONVILLE FFRENCH-BEYTAGH

REFINER'S FIRE,
MY HEART'S ONE DESIRE
IS TO BE HOLY,
SET APART FOR YOU, LORD.
I CHOOSE TO BE HOLY,
SET APART FOR YOU,
MY MASTER,
READY TO DO YOUR WILL.

(From the song *Purify my heart* by Brian Doerksen, © 1990 Mercy/Vineyard Publishing)

HOW CAN WE SUPPORT THOSE IMPRISONED AT THE MOMENT FOR THEIR FAITH?

Sixteenth Sunday in Ordinary Time

Thought for the day

Like a good shepherd, Jesus sees the needs of his people and always responds with love.

Readings

Jeremiah 23:1–6
Ephesians 2:13–18
Mark 6:30–34

Aim: To see how Jesus' ministry as leader and shepherd fulfilled the prophecies.

Starter

What's my line? Take turns miming a job while the others try to figure out what job it is.

Teaching

Begin by reading what God thought of the job being done by the leaders of his people during the time of Jeremiah, not long before they were taken off into Babylon as exiles. On the sheet there is space to jot down the reasons why God is going to punish these irresponsible leaders. Also draw attention to the love God has for his people as he talks of a future leader who will take proper care of them. That would be quite a job, and only one person could do it.

Look next at the gospel to see Jesus in action, and the passage from Ephesians. Jot down what everyone notices about his ministry, as if you are compiling a job description. (For example: on call 24 hours a day; no guaranteed regular vacation time. Accommodation and food variable according to availability and others' hospitality; salary $00.00. Highly demanding but highly rewarding work.)

Praying

The Lord is my shepherd,
I have everything I need.
He gives me rest in green pastures.
He leads me to calm water.
He gives me new strength.
True to his name
he leads me on paths that are right.

(From Psalm 23)

Activities

There is space on the activity sheet to record the needs of God's people, suffering under bad leaders, and the practical loving shepherding that Jesus provides, reflecting the Father's love. They are encouraged to imagine what such a ministry would feel like as a disciple, as Jesus himself, and as someone among the crowds.

Discussion starters

1. Jesus tried to ensure that his disciples had times of rest and spiritual refreshment. Do we follow that example in our church community?
2. Why were the crowds going out of their way to flock to Jesus?

Notes

Seventeenth Sunday in Ordinary Time

Thought for the day

Out of God's riches, a great crowd is fed and satisfied from a small offering of food.

Readings

2 Kings 4:42–44
Ephesians 4:1–6
John 6:1–15

Aim: To see how this feeding prefigures the feeding of the Last Supper and the Eucharist.

Starter

Bring a selection of breads from different parts of the world, together with an atlas or world map. Find where each bread comes from and sample it. All over the world bread of some kind is basic food.

Teaching

Begin by reading the passage from 2 Kings, where Elisha feeds a hundred people with a gift of bread. Notice the generosity (in offering the bread) and Elisha's careful listening to God's will, and his wholehearted obedience to it.

Now look at the feeding of the five thousand in John's gospel. Draw attention to the timing—it's about Passover time. (Another meal, just before the escape from slavery.) Look at what Jesus does with the food—he accepts the gift, gives thanks to God for it, breaks it in pieces and gives it out to the people to feed them when they are hungry.

Link this with what Jesus started at the Passover meal he shared with his disciples before his death, and which goes on happening in all our churches right through the centuries and the generations, all over the world. That is quite a crowd being fed! And we are part of that same blessing, breaking and giving out, which has been going on for about two thousand years. It's a record-breaking meal.

Praying

(From Ephesians 3, a prayer to pray for each other)

I pray that Christ will live in your hearts
because of your faith.
I pray that your life will be strong in love
and built on love.
And I pray that you and all God's holy people
will have the power to understand
the greatness of Christ's love—
how wide and high, long and deep that love is.

Activities

On the activity sheet there are pictures of Christians from different times in history and different countries, all taking part in God's feeding program. The actions of Jesus are linked with what happens in church at the Eucharist.

Discussion starters

1. When faced with our next problem which looks insurmountable, how can today's gospel help us do things God's way?

2. Why do you think John mentions that the feeding of the five thousand takes place at the time of the Jewish Passover? What other meal would Jesus preside over at Passover?

Notes

THE FEEDING GOES ON AND ON...
5 LOAVES AND 2 FISHES WASN'T MUCH TO START WITH, WAS IT?

Not in itself, no. But it was one person's willingness to be generous, and God can do a lot with that.

SO IF I OFFERED MY LIFE, EVEN THOUGH I'M ONLY ONE PERSON AND ONLY ME, COULD GOD USE THAT GIFT IN THE SAME WAY?

Yes! And when you get to heaven you'll see just how many people were blessed through your giving!

WHAT CAN I GIVE?

HOW DOES GOD FEED US?

OUR WORLD IS HUNGRY   MARK 14:22   MATTHEW 4:4   JOHN 6:48

JESUS TOOK WHAT WAS OFFERED   GAVE THANKS TO GOD   BROKE IT UP   AND GAVE IT OUT TO THE PEOPLE

I PRAY THAT CHRIST WILL LIVE IN YOUR HEARTS BECAUSE OF YOUR FAITH. I PRAY THAT YOUR LIFE WILL BE STRONG IN LOVE AND BUILT ON LOVE. AND I PRAY THAT YOU AND ALL GOD'S HOLY PEOPLE WILL HAVE THE POWER TO UNDERSTAND THE GREATNESS OF CHRIST'S LOVE — HOW WIDE AND HIGH, LONG AND DEEP THAT LOVE IS.   —AMEN—
(FROM EPHESIANS 3, TO PRAY FOR EACH OTHER)

Eighteenth Sunday in Ordinary Time

Thought for the day

Jesus is the Bread of Life who satisfies our hunger and sustains us on our journey to heaven.

Readings

Exodus 16:2–4, 12–15
Ephesians 4:17, 20–24
John 6:24–35

Aim: To explore the significance of Jesus describing himself as the Bread of Life.

Starter

This person… Sit in a circle, and take turns describing someone (who may be famous, or someone everyone knows), not by looks but by different things they do or have done. Whoever guesses the identity can have the next go.

Teaching

We managed to work out who those people were without knowing anything about their appearance. We know hardly anything about Jesus' appearance, but we can tell a great deal about him by what he said and did. Today we're going to look at one of the ways Jesus described himself.

Read today's gospel, writing "I am the Bread of Life" on a large sheet as it comes up. Talk about what Jesus might have meant by this. (Look at what bread does for our physical bodies and then look at how Jesus does this in a spiritual way, especially in the gift of Holy Communion—feeding, satisfying hunger, providing essentials for growth and health and energy, and so on.)

Now look back to the Exodus passage and Psalm 78, referred to in the gospel, so that they can see the connection and the background to the way Jesus was thinking. Who did the people think had provided them with manna in the desert? (Look at Jesus' reply in John 6:32.) Remembering how the crowd had just recently been miraculously fed by Jesus, talk about what they might have meant in verse 30 of John 6. What does it mean to "believe in the one God sent"? (Verse 29)

Point out that we all walk straight past things we're not prepared or expecting to see, and some of the people couldn't believe that Jesus could be anywhere near as holy as Moses, the holy figure from the past. They didn't realize that Moses had been pointing toward this moment, and that they happened to be alive at the very time God's Son came to the earth.

Finally, look at Ephesians, where we are shown how this risen life, nourished by the Bread of Life, works out in practice. Notice anything they recognize from their own experience of Christians, and anything which they feel our own community is falling short on.

Praying

Lord Jesus Christ,
I would come to you,
live my life for you,
Son of God.
All your commands I know are true,
your many gifts will make me new,
into my life your power breaks through,
living Lord.

(Taken from the song *Lord Jesus Christ* by Patrick Appleford © 1960 Josef Weinberger)

Activities

On the activity sheet today's teaching is reinforced with space to record the qualities of bread which help us understand about the nature of Jesus. They are also helped to see the links between God's feeding of his people in the desert and our feeding as a travelling people.

Discussion starters

1. Do we realize our need of Jesus' feeding, or think of it more as an optional extra?

2. How can our God-given work in life just be to believe in Jesus? (What difference does that belief make to everything else we do?)

Notes

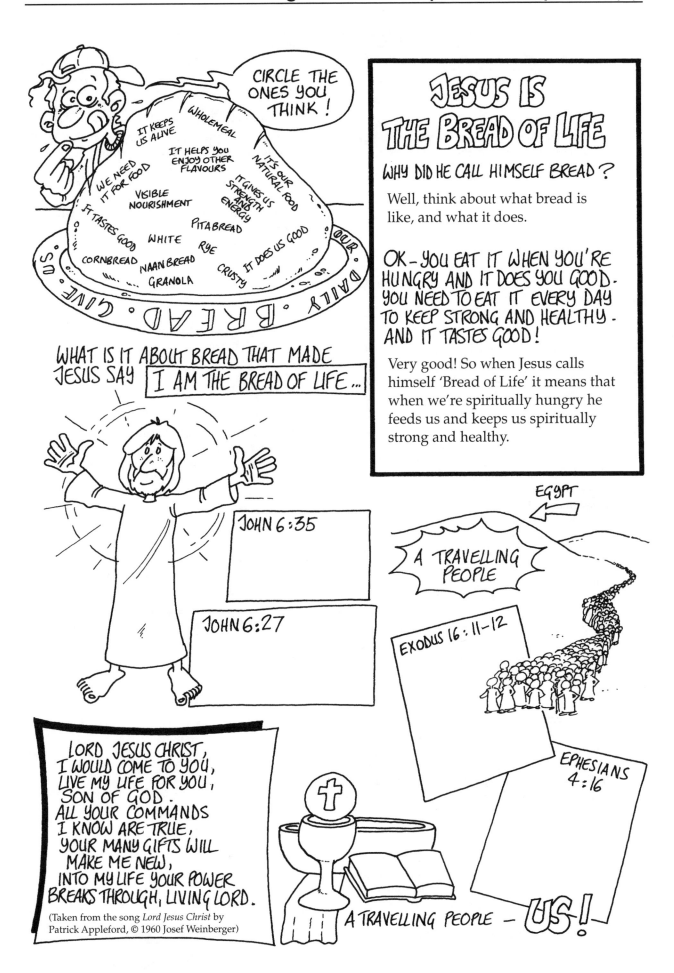

CIRCLE THE ONES YOU THINK!

IT KEEPS US ALIVE · WHOLEMEAL · IT'S OUR NATURAL FOOD · IT HELPS YOU ENJOY OTHER FLAVOURS · WE NEED IT FOR FOOD · IT GIVES US STRENGTH AND ENERGY · VISIBLE NOURISHMENT · IT TASTES GOOD · PITA BREAD · WHITE · RYE · IT DOES US GOOD · CORNBREAD · NAAN BREAD · GRANOLA · CRUSTY

OUR · DAILY · BREAD · GIVE · US

JESUS IS THE BREAD OF LIFE

WHY DID HE CALL HIMSELF BREAD?

Well, think about what bread is like, and what it does.

OK — YOU EAT IT WHEN YOU'RE HUNGRY AND IT DOES YOU GOOD. YOU NEED TO EAT IT EVERY DAY TO KEEP STRONG AND HEALTHY. AND IT TASTES GOOD!

Very good! So when Jesus calls himself 'Bread of Life' it means that when we're spiritually hungry he feeds us and keeps us spiritually strong and healthy.

WHAT IS IT ABOUT BREAD THAT MADE JESUS SAY I AM THE BREAD OF LIFE...

JOHN 6:35

JOHN 6:27

EGYPT

A TRAVELLING PEOPLE

EXODUS 16:11-12

EPHESIANS 4:16

LORD JESUS CHRIST, I WOULD COME TO YOU, LIVE MY LIFE FOR YOU, SON OF GOD. ALL YOUR COMMANDS I KNOW ARE TRUE, YOUR MANY GIFTS WILL MAKE ME NEW, INTO MY LIFE YOUR POWER BREAKS THROUGH, LIVING LORD.

(Taken from the song *Lord Jesus Christ* by Patrick Appleford, © 1960 Josef Weinberger)

A TRAVELLING PEOPLE — US!

Nineteenth Sunday in Ordinary Time

Thought for the day

Just as bread is the visible form of life-giving nourishment, so Jesus is the visible form of God's life-giving love.

Readings

1 Kings 19:4–8
Ephesians 4:30—5:2
John 6:41–51

Aim: To explore ways in which we can read God's signs.

Starter

Use the road signs on page 127 and write up the "spiritual" meanings separately. Hang them up around the walls. Send everyone around to match them up.

Teaching

Read the passage from 1 Kings 19, where Elijah is provided with the rest, food and drink he needs to continue in God's calling. Elijah is exhausted and depressed as he walks into the desert, and he recognizes that God is providing for him in the shady tree, the much-needed sleep, the bread and the water. He understands these things as signs of God's love, because he is already used to being attentive to God and expecting God to communicate with him. Too often we don't notice God's care of us through the ordinary things of life, but actually every meal, every shower when we're hot and sticky, every clean bed we collapse into, every patch of shade …all of these ordinary, everyday things are signs to us of God's love for us, and we just take it all for granted, unless we've recently had to do without such luxuries! God's practical provision enables us to do the work he calls us into.

Jesus' commission is to be our Savior, acting out God's total love in words and actions throughout his life. Sometimes this must have been uplifting and thrilling, as great crowds began to understand how God was reaching out to them. But at other times the message had to continue to be proclaimed in the face of hostility, as in today's gospel. (Read that now.)

Jesus is claiming a very special relationship with God, which has been backed up by signs and miracles of many different kinds. The stage is set for the religious leaders to hail him as the true Messiah, for whom they have been waiting for generations, and towards whom Moses and the prophets had carefully directed their hearers and readers.

But the religious leaders cannot and do not read the signs.

Now read the passage from Ephesians, which gives some excellent advice for keeping ourselves ready to notice God's signs. It is all to do with regularly cleaning up after ourselves, recognizing that we need to check our position and direction with God, several times in each day. Knowing God's love for us has the effect of making us actually want to keep coming back like this—we do it not out of fear or a burdensome duty, but out of love and gratitude, knowing that so much more of the positives can happen, and life feels right when we are right with God.

Praying

A man that looks on glass,
on it may stay his eye;
or, if he chooses, through it pass,
and thus the heavens espy.
Lord, in all the outward things,
let me see you and learn from you.
Amen.

Activities

On the activity sheet there are various signs to read, and they are encouraged to read the signs of the natural world which tell us of God's nature. They also look at some of the everyday signs of God's practical caring, linking Elijah's feeding with Jesus coming to us as "Bread from heaven."

Discussion starters

1. Are we aware of when we are listening to learn and understand, and when we are not? Do we really want to hear whatever God says to us?

2. Are we taking Jesus up on his offer of feeding, and relying on it for dear life, or do we tend to glance at the Bread of Life but commit ourselves to spiritual junk food—or spiritual starvation?

Notes

WHAT DO THESE SIGNS MEAN ???

READING GOD'S SIGNS

WHAT SORT OF SIGNS DOES GOD GIVE US TO READ? Well, there's the universe – everything we know and live in, everything we see and hear, and all the invisible things, too.

WHAT DO THEY ALL MEAN? That depends on what God wants to show us. One day you might see heavy rain which makes you realize how God showers and soaks us with his love. Another day the rain might remind us of how God shares the sadness and suffering of our world.

HOW DO I KNOW IT'S GOD SPEAKING AND NOT JUST MY OWN THOUGHTS? Good question. God does talk to us through our thoughts but he is always true to his nature. So if the thoughts are selfish, unloving or dishonest, they are not of God. If they match up with God's nature, they probably are God speaking to you.

GOD'S FAITHFULNESS AND RELIABILITY

GOD'S POWER

HOW CAN THINGS IN OUR WORLD SHOW US...

GOD'S ORDER AND ATTENTION TO DETAIL

GOD'S IMAGINATION AND HUMOUR

O LORD, LET ME DIE!

WHAT ORDINARY THINGS DID GOD USE TO HELP ELIJAH GO ON?

"I AM THE LIVING BREAD"

"A MAN THAT LOOKS ON GLASS, ON IT MAY STAY HIS EYE; OR IF HE CHOOSES, THROUGH IT PASS AND THUS THE HEAVENS ESPY." LORD, IN ALL THE OUTWARD THINGS, LET ME SEE YOU AND LEARN FROM YOU.
—AMEN—

WHAT ORDINARY WAYS DOES GOD USE TO SHOW US HIS LOVING CARE?

Twentieth Sunday in Ordinary Time

Thought for the day

God's wisdom may appear foolishness without the God-given grace to understand.

Readings

Proverbs 9:1–6
Ephesians 5:15–20
John 6:51–58

Aim: To see how God's wisdom is sometimes seen as foolishness.

Starter

Sing one of those silly songs with actions, such as "Did you ever see a zombie come to tea? Take a look at me—a zombie you will see." With each verse an extra action is added: marching with feet, right arm up and down, left arm up and down, nod head, blink.

Teaching

Now we have all made ourselves look ridiculous! Today we are going to look at how God's wisdom is often seen as complete foolishness. Perhaps they have already been made to feel foolish for believing in God and talking to him. It is never a nice experience, and can set us wondering why we bother with God if it's going to make some people laugh at us and think we're stupid. (Of course, God is there whether we bother with him or not, so it won't make God disappear if we deny him. Nor will it help those who are doing the scoffing. But we do need to support one another with our prayers, and to know that Jesus received the same scorn from his contemporaries.)

Read the passage from Proverbs, telling them also about the lady Folly, in contrast to Wisdom. At first sight Folly can look like a good idea, appealing to our instincts and cravings, rather like much of the media does today. Only after people have made their choice is it clear that this leads to death, whereas the path of Wisdom leads to life-giving nourishment and fulfillment.

Go on to read the passage from Ephesians, discussing what "living wisely" means for us. Draw out the need to be actively involved in goodness, rather than just not doing anyone any harm.

Now look at today's gospel, where the religious leaders are finding it impossible to see Jesus' words as wisdom, but only as foolishness and blasphemy. What keeps them from seeing the truth of Jesus' words? (Look at their expectations of the Messiah, their attention to precise detail at the expense of the wider vision, and their status as learned, respected leaders in the community.)

Praying

Be thou my wisdom, be thou my true word,
I ever with thee and thou with me, Lord;
thou my great Father, and I thy true heir;
thou in me dwelling, and I in thy care.

(From a song translated from the Irish
by Mary Byrne and Eleanor Hull
© Copyright Control)

Activities

On the activity sheet they are helped to look at some of the things that those who cannot accept God find foolish, and to see how they are in fact wisdom, though contrasting with the world's values. They are also encouraged to see how they can live wisely, making the most of every opportunity to do good and fight against evil.

Discussion starters

1. What is the difference between being clever, learned and knowledgeable, and being wise?

2. Why do learned and clever people often find it harder to understand God's wisdom? Should this affect the way our children are "taught"?

Notes

THE SON OF GOD BEING A CARPENTER FROM NAZARETH

THE GREAT AND AWESOME G-O-D WALKING ABOUT AMONG ORDINARY PEOPLE

THE MESSIAH MAKING FRIENDS WITH THE RIFF RAFF OF SOCIETY

THE MESSIAH SHOWING UP THE RELIGIOUS TEACHERS OF THE SACRED LAW AS HYPOCRITES

THIS CAN'T BE GOD'S WISDOM — WE THINK IT'S TOTAL FOOLISHNESS!

WISDOM v. FOOLISHNESS

HOW CAN WISDOM BE FOOLISHNESS, OR THE OTHER WAY ROUND FOR THAT MATTER?

It all depends where you're standing. Some people would consider it wise to go walking in the mountains all day, others would think it a foolish waste of energy.

SO IS IT THE SAME WITH GOD'S WISDOM?

Yes, only more so. It might seem wise to spoil yourself and insist on your own way, but living against God's Law of love is foolishness in the long term.

WHAT IS WISDOM, THEN?

Seeking out God's will for us and our world, and living in harmony with the One who designed us.

PUT A SQUARE ROUND GOD'S WISDOM/WORLD'S FOOLISHNESS

PUT A CIRCLE ROUND THE WORLD'S IDEA OF WISDOM

BE THOU MY WISDOM, BE THOU MY TRUE WORD, I EVER WITH THEE AND THOU WITH ME, LORD; THOU MY GREAT FATHER AND I THY TRUE HEIR; THOU IN ME DWELLING, AND I IN THY CARE.

(From a song translated from the Irish by Mary Byrne and Eleanor Hull, © Copyright Control)

ALWAYS LOOK AFTER NUMBER 1 AT ALL COSTS.

PUT YOURSELF OUT FOR OTHERS, LOVING THEM.

AIM TO IMPRESS OTHER PEOPLE SO THEY RESPECT YOU AND VALUE YOU.

WHAT YOU LOOK LIKE AND BUY IS EXTREMELY IMPORTANT.

TO BE BEAUTIFUL IN GOD'S EYES HAS NOTHING TO DO WITH HOW YOU LOOK.

STOP WORRYING ABOUT WHAT IMPRESSES PEOPLE AND LEARN TO SEEK GOD'S WILL.

Twenty-first Sunday in Ordinary Time

Thought for the day

"To whom else could we go? You alone have the words of eternal life."

Readings

Joshua 24:1–2a, 15–18
Ephesians 5:21–32
John 6:60–69

Aim: To explore why the split happened at this point.

Starter

Why? (This is a variation on *Call my bluff*.) Split the group into two teams and give each some kind of bell or other noise item. Whoever is first with the right choice wins the round. Here are some ideas to get you started.

1. Why did the campanologist climb the stairs? (a) because he was camping at the top of a mountain; (b) because he was campaigning in high-rise flats; (c) because the bells he was ringing were in a tower.

2. Why was the kleptomaniac arrested? (a) because she was a compulsive clog dancer; (b) because she was a compulsive thief; (c) because she was a compulsive stalker.

3. Why did Jeremiah not have sore armpits? (a) because his friends padded them with rags; (b) because he never shaved them; (c) because he used Oil of Olay every day.

4. Why did the student need his portfolio? (a) because he was going to sea; (b) because he wanted to choose some wine to celebrate passing his exams; (c) because his artwork was carried in it.

Teaching

Why do we do the things we do? Often there isn't just one reason but lots of little reasons and events that come together. (Why, for instance, is each person here today?) Today we are looking at people making important decisions, and why they made them.

Read the passage from Joshua, with the people's choice based on their personal experience of Yahweh's care and their trust in what Joshua, their leader, advises. Then read the gospel for today. Why did they find what Jesus was saying so hard that it made them decide to walk no more with him? Share ideas about this, and help them to see that in making those statements, Jesus was saying that he was the Holy One of God, and this was a very hard thing to accept, especially for Jewish people who thought of God as so awesome that they never even allowed themselves to say his name. The thought of the transcendent God walking among them in sandals was mind blowing, so they came to the conclusion that Jesus must either have gone "over the top" or was a liar.

But if he really was telling the truth—and all the evidence pointed to that—then God's Son was actually standing with them, breathing the same air.

Praying

Yes, Lord, I believe that you are the Christ,
the Son of God who has come into the world.
I have decided to follow you,
for you alone have the words of eternal life.

Activities

On the activity sheet there are different reasons for believing that the world is flat/round. They can use these to see how we come to conclusions which others would challenge unless they have plenty of evidence. They then compare Peter and the disciples' reasons for concluding that Jesus is the Holy One of God, compared with those who turn away.

Discussion starters

1. What do we actually believe Jesus to be, and how does this affect our life?

2. Why do you think Jesus made no attempt to persuade those who turned away to return?

Notes

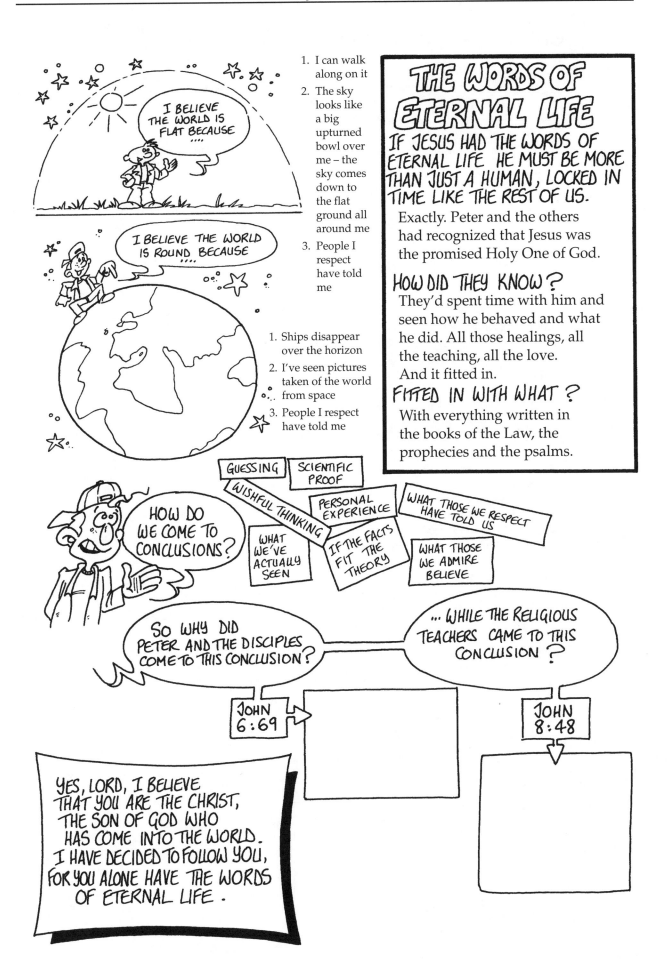

Twenty-second Sunday in Ordinary Time

Thought for the day

We need to be careful never to replace the timeless commands of God with man-made traditions.

Readings

Deuteronomy 4:1–2, 6–8
James 1:17–18, 21–22, 27
Mark 7:1–8, 14–15, 21–23

Aim: To look at the benefits and dangers of tradition in the church.

Starter

On separate index cards write down various traditions that they sort into "Very important," "Non-essential" and "Discard." Here are some ideas: Christmas pudding; a white wedding; wearing black at funerals; school uniform; dinner before dessert; milk poured in before the tea; standing for the national anthem; salt and vinegar with chips; homework; wearing best clothes to church; ladies first.

Teaching

Lots of our traditions are so much a part of life that we only notice them when we travel abroad and find they're not there. Sometimes we take it for granted that anything we're used to doing must be right. Today we're going to look at that and question it, as Jesus did.

First read the passage from Deuteronomy, reminding them of the basic principles of the Law—Love God and love one another. Make a list of the advantages of having traditions in place to help keep the Law. Use the sheet to see how the extra "fence" of rules and regulations became part of the tradition, from the best of motives, but having the effect of shifting priorities in people's minds.

Now read the gospel passage from Mark 7, picking out the dangers and disadvantages of having intricately worked-out traditional customs. What had happened to the way the people thought of religious duty?

Finally, talk over the traditions of our own church, looking at what is obviously very precious and important, and what seems to them to be rather in line with some of the religious teachers' rules and regulations.

Praying

Lord, I want to show my love and thanks
in the way I live my life.
I want everything I think, say and do
to be in line with your Law of love.
Lord, help me to be more concerned
with the state of my soul before you,
than with my efforts to impress other people.
Amen.

Activities

There is space on the activity sheet to work out quantities of time, energy and money spent on various things in life, in order to assess what our life is actually displaying. And they are helped to see how the build-up of regulations grew out of a genuine desire to keep the Law faithfully.

Discussion starters

1. Is there anything in the church today—which is the Body of Christ—that Jesus might be unhappy with?

2. Do we still accept Jesus' teaching that the "uncleanliness" which so often leads to sin comes from the inside of people, or is responsibility for sin being replaced by genetics and other circumstances beyond our control?

Notes

Twenty-third Sunday in Ordinary Time

Thought for the day

Jesus comes fulfilling the hope of healing to wholeness; he shows that mercy has triumphed over judgment.

Readings

Isaiah 35:4–7a
James 2:1–5
Mark 7:31–37

Aim: To look at the Christian attitude toward prejudice and discrimination.

Starter

Size, shape, color. All work together (or in smaller groups) on the puzzle shown below. No adjoining shapes can have more than one thing in common.

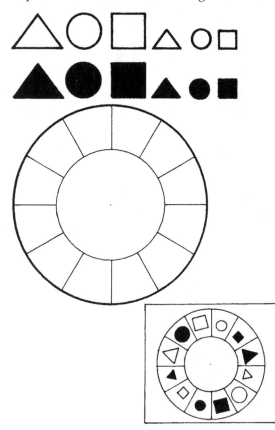

Teaching

Being able to discriminate between things is an important skill which we need to have. But often our society is full of discrimination of the wrong sort, selecting those who are acceptable and those who are not; those we respect and those we can despise. There's also lots of prejudice (the word means judging before you've even met) and

today's readings help us discover what Jesus' views are.

First read the prophecy from Isaiah, noticing the wide-ranging healing it describes, with nothing and no one excluded or shut off by physical disabilities.

Then read the passage from James, looking out for some advice for us about discrimination and prejudice. As one of the proverbs says, the thing that rich and poor have in common is that God made them both! This passage challenges our attitudes as individuals, as the church and as members of a nation. Draw attention to mercy triumphing over judgment.

Now read the gospel for today. This is the story of a man who was shut off, or excluded, before being welcomed in, through the silence of hearing loss. Notice how the prophecy is being fulfilled without Jesus forcing things to happen, but simply responding to needs as they present themselves. Mercy has triumphed over judgment.

Praying

Father we pray for all who are cut off
from the world of sight and hearing,
and for those who just feel
cut off and left out.
Jesus didn't leave anyone out.
Teach us to live that way too.
Amen.

Activities

On the activity sheet there are various hot topics to look at in the church and in society concerning discrimination and prejudice. The children are helped to look at these in the light of the gospel. They are drawing up a few guidelines for challenging the rest of us as well, and these could perhaps be printed in a magazine or the local newspaper.

Discussion starters

1. Can we appreciate mercy unless we first appreciate the judgment we deserve?
2. How do we stand, as church and as a nation, in relation to issues of discrimination and prejudice?

Notes

MERCY HAS TRIUMPHED OVER JUDGEMENT

MERCY MEANS LETTING YOU OFF—RIGHT?
Right. It's not excusing you, and pretending you weren't wrong. It's knowing you were in the wrong and letting you off anyway.

LIKE BEING LET OFF A BAD DEBT?
Yes. God gives us forgiveness for free, and we're to do the same, forgiving other people instead of harboring grudges.

SOMETIMES PEOPLE HARBOUR GRUDGES FOR NO REASON AT ALL, DON'T THEY?
Sadly, yes. Our world is full of people who are shut out by prejudice and discrimination.

WHAT CAN WE DO AS CHRISTIANS?
Aim to live free of prejudice, respecting every other human being as a child of God.

Twenty-fourth Sunday in Ordinary Time

Thought for the day

Loving obedience to God is shown by Jesus to be a quality rich in courage and wisdom, a quality to be highly respected.

Readings

Isaiah 50:5–9
James 2:14–18
Mark 8:27–35

Aim: To explore the value and importance of Jesus' loving obedience, and its implications for us as his followers.

Starter

Collect some snails and stage a snail race down a premarked sheet of 8 1/2 x11 paper.

Teaching

However much we shouted encouragement at our snails, they weren't able to be particularly obedient either to us, or the ruled lines marking their lanes. They still have no idea of what they were supposed to be doing. Today we are going to look at what obedience really is.

Begin by reading the passage from Isaiah 50, describing God's obedient Servant, willing to go along with God's guidance even in the face of violent opposition. Who does it sound like? For us, living after Jesus' coming, the passage points very significantly to Jesus, describing the kind of loving obedience he showed during all his life and particularly in his trial and crucifixion. This kind of obedience came from the way Jesus was always so close to his Father—at one with him, so that God's will was also Jesus' will.

Now look at today's gospel from Mark 8. Jesus is making it plain that part of being the Christ is the necessity to go through the suffering foretold by the prophets. That loving obedience is all part of Jesus' identity as the Messiah, or holy, anointed One of God. And Jesus goes further; it's also part of being someone who claims to be one of Christ's followers, like us. If we mean what we say, it will involve a daily willingness to walk the way of the cross (verse 34).

Have the words of the Lord's Prayer available, and draw their attention to the way the first section of the prayer is placing ourselves in that loving obedience, whenever we say, "Let your kingdom come; let your will be done on earth as it is in heaven." Do we realize what we are saying here? We need to do that conscious placing of ourselves in obedience to God every single time we say those words—and say them at least morning, afternoon and evening every day.

Praying

Our Father, who art in heaven,
hallowed be thy name;
thy kingdom come;
thy will be done on earth as it is in heaven.

Activities

On the activity sheet there is an example of how the tongue can be a powerful instrument for spreading both trouble and good. Examples of Jesus' loving obedience are used to help us in our obedience, and they are encouraged to work out what obedience involves.

Discussion starters

1. Has the time come to take another look at obedience and see if we've grown up enough to consider it a Godly quality worth developing?
2. Why does Jesus say that following him is bound to involve taking up our cross as he did?

Notes

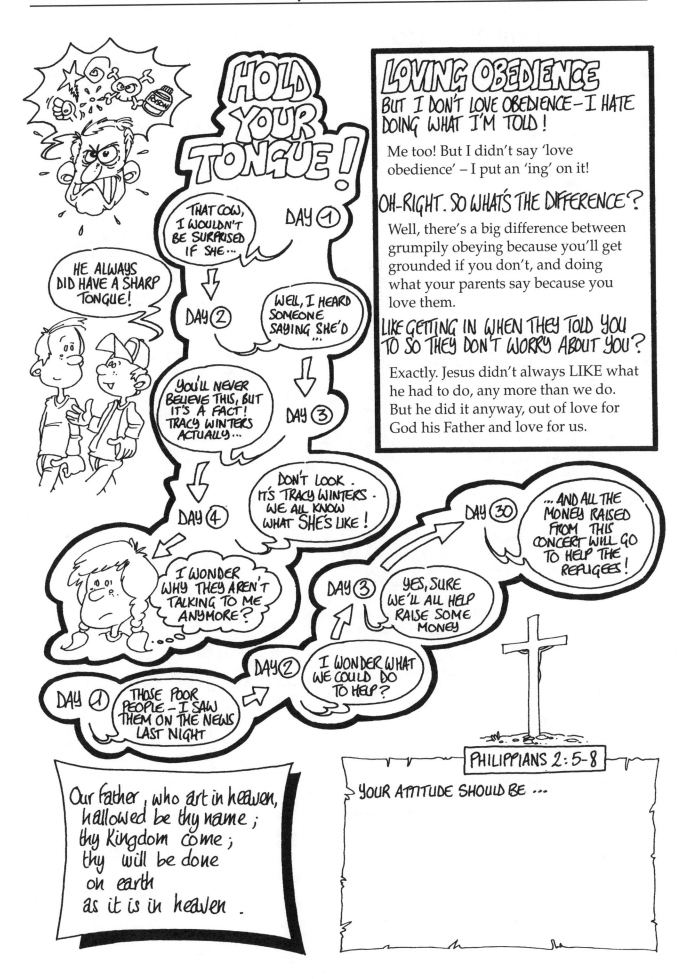

Twenty-fifth Sunday in Ordinary Time

Thought for the day

The truly great in God's eyes are those who are prepared to be last of all and servant of all.

Readings

Wisdom 2:12, 17–20
James 3:16—4:3
Mark 9:30–37

Aim: To understand Jesus' teaching about greatness and servanthood.

Starter

Have a number of pictures of famous people from newspapers and magazines cut out and stuck around the room, numbered. Give out sheets of paper. Everyone goes around writing down the names of those pictured. The one with most right gets to wear a posh hat to show how clever they are.

Teaching

All the people in those pictures were famous, for all sorts of reasons. They were all "the greatest" in their particular area. Now read today's gospel, where the disciples have been arguing about which of them should be the greatest. Why were they ashamed to admit to Jesus what they had been talking about? Why might their argument have disturbed Jesus? (He knew that they were going to be the leaders of the church, and here they were behaving like pagan leaders, full of boasting and jealousy.) Notice how Jesus both explains and shows them, with the little child, what he means. Children were vulnerable, and with no status at all, so to accept Jesus by accepting them suggests that he is prepared to think of himself on a level with what most people would consider the very lowest of the low. (How do we choose our friends? Would we feel embarrassed to be seen with some people because our other friends despise them?)

Now read the passage from James. There are more arguments here, and James is helping his hearers understand where all this strife comes from. That makes it easier to sort out, provided we genuinely want it sorted. Sometimes people enjoy having their battles and moans. Look at the sound advice James gives. He helps us see that Satan fools us into thinking he's big and powerful, but if we really stand our ground and fix our feet in what we know is right and good, Satan's power trickles out of him, and he slinks away. This is a very useful image for when we find ourselves being tempted, and it always works.

Praying

The world wants the wealth to live in state,
but you show us a new way to be great:
like a servant you came
and if we do the same
we'll be turning the world upside down.

(Taken from the song *O Lord, all the world* by Patrick Appleford © 1965 Josef Weinberger)

Activities

There is a short sketch to look at the reasons for arguments, linked with the James reading, and some information about status so that they can better grasp what Jesus is saying in today's gospel. There are some different life ambitions to consider.

Discussion starters

1. Why does Jesus use a child as a focus for talking about greatness?

2. Look at examples of arguments and strife—personally, locally and internationally—and see if they do come from what Jesus and James suggest.

Notes

- Can I have a turn now?
- No.
- Oh, come on, you've been on it for hours.
- Yeah, I know. It's mine, remember?
- Well, you're mean, hogging it all the time.
  I only want a little turn.
- Shut up and go away. This level's really hard and I
  need to concentrate.
- Well, I hope the hard drive crashes, then. And don't
  expect to borrow my bike tomorrow.

WHAT CAUSES ARGUMENTS?

King   We need more land.

Queen We could take some from the country
next door, dearest.

King   Mmm, yes, good idea. I've been
meaning to get my own back on
them for polluting our rivers.

Queen Shall I call the chief army commander
for you then, dear?

King   Yes – we'll build up forces on our side
to frighten them, and when they shoot
at us we'll blast in and flatten them!

Queen More tea, dear?

LOWEST OF THE LOW

WHO IS ?

That depends what age you live in,
and which culture. But it's those who
have no rights, no influence and very
little money, and most people have
little respect for them.

WHO WAS THAT IN JESUS' TIME ?

Slaves, servants, women and children,
plus the social outcasts.

**SO WHEN JESUS USED A YOUNG CHILD
AS AN EXAMPLE IT WASN'T FOR
THE "AH, HOW CUTE" VALUE ?**

Exactly. He was showing them
someone considered lacking all
power and status.

**AND WE'RE TO THINK OF OURSELVES
AS SERVING EVEN THEM !**

You've got it.

SELFISHNESS   ENVY   HOLDING GRUDGES

JEALOUSY   GREED

THINKING WE ARE MORE IMPORTANT THAN OTHERS

THINKING WE DESERVE MORE THAN OTHERS

WANTING WHAT ISN'T OURS

HOW CAN WE GET TO A WIN/WIN SITUATION ?

THE WORLD WANTS THE WEALTH TO LIVE IN STATE,
BUT YOU SHOW US A NEW WAY TO BE GREAT:
LIKE A SERVANT YOU CAME
AND IF WE DO THE SAME
WE'LL BE TURNING THE WORLD UPSIDE DOWN.

(Taken from the song *O Lord, all the world* by Patrick Appleford
© 1965 Josef Weinberger)

Twenty-sixth Sunday in Ordinary Time

Thought for the day
Don't let your body lead you into sin and risk exchanging eternal life for eternal punishment.

Readings
Numbers 11:25–29
James 5:1–6
Mark 9:38–43, 45, 47–48

Aim: To look at the importance of being prepared for temptation.

Starter
Press flour into a pudding dish with a coin somewhere inside and carefully upend it so you have a pudding-shape of flour. People take turns at slicing the "pudding" without making it collapse, and without dislodging the coin. Continue until one of those things happens, and the one who was cutting a slice at the time has to clear it all away. But they can keep the coin!

Teaching
Today we're looking at resisting temptation. If we're not well prepared for it, we're more likely to find our good intentions collapsing in a cloud of dust, like our flour pudding. We're taking temptation seriously because Jesus did. He was tempted very severely just after his Baptism, during his ministry and in the garden of Gethsemane, just before he was arrested, and he urgently warned his disciples to watch and pray so that they wouldn't give way to temptation. They didn't realize how important it was, and ended up scattering, and leaving Jesus when he most needed them.

Begin by reading today's gospel, from Mark 9, picking up on how seriously Jesus is wanting us to take this teaching. He uses strong, violent examples to make us think, and to help us recognize what a real battle it can be to resist evil; it isn't something to treat casually because the effects are so lasting and so damaging, both to ourselves and others, not just in this life but after death as well. Jesus is suggesting that we take strong action to turn our backs on temptation before it drags us into sin. As soon as a sin looks attractive to us—tempting—our danger lights should start flashing and that's when we need to take action. If we don't, the temptation will just get stronger, and harder to resist. Temptation is well worth resisting because sin is long-term destructive.

Now look at the passage from Numbers, seeing how temptation works on the people, and the trouble it causes. Also notice the link between Joshua's protest and the disciples' protest in Mark

9:38, and the similarity between Moses' and Jesus' replies.

Praying
The dearest idol I have known,
whatever that idol be,
help me to tear it from thy throne
and worship only thee.

Activities
On the activity sheet the passage from James draws attention to faithful prayer and its effectiveness. There is also a diagram showing how temptation works and how we can short circuit it in God's strength.

Discussion starters
1. Do we believe that prayer is truly effective or not? If not, what may be blocking the power?
2. Jesus is very serious about not leading the vulnerable into sin. What can we actively do in our society as those concerned for the eternal well-being of souls?

Notes

HOW DOES TEMPTATION WORK?

THAT'S FANTASTIC. I WANT IT.

← YOU CAN'T AFFORD IT.

I WANT IT.

YOU CAN HAVE IT IF YOU STEAL THE MONEY ⇒   ⇐ IT'S WRONG TO STEAL

I WANT IT.

IT'S NOT REALLY STEALING — YOU CAN PAY IT BACK ONE DAY ⇒   ⇐ IT'S STEALING AND STEALING'S WRONG

I WANT IT !

YOU CAN SHORT-CIRCUIT TEMPTATION MORE EASILY BEFORE IT'S GROWN HUGE, SO STAMP ON IT STRAIGHT AWAY!

RESISTING TEMPTATION

I'M NOT VERY GOOD AT THAT.

Have you ever thought about why it's so difficult?

WELL, YOU'RE ONLY TEMPTED TO DO AND SAY THINGS THAT YOU WANT TO, REALLY BADLY. THAT'S THE TROUBLE.

Yes, that's right. So we need to be ready for it.

HOW DO YOU MEAN?

If you know you're going to malaria countries you take malaria tablets.

SO WHAT CAN I TAKE TO PROTECT ME AGAINST FALLING INTO TEMPTATION?   God's protection.

Put on his armor of prayer, faith and righteousness, and be prepared!

PRAY FOR THOSE BEING TEMPTED

REALLY LONG FOR THEM TO BE STRONG

ASK GOD'S PROTECTION FOR THEM

YOUR PRAYER _DOES_ MAKE A DIFFERENCE

"A good person's prayer is very powerful and effective" JAMES 5:16

THE DEAREST IDOL I HAVE KNOWN, WHATEVER THAT IDOL BE, HELP ME TO TEAR IT FROM THY THRONE AND WORSHIP ONLY THEE.

TEMPTATION ZONE

WHERE ARE MINE?

Twenty-seventh Sunday in Ordinary Time

Thought for the day

Human beings are made responsible for the care of creation but are subject to God in all aspects of their lives.

Readings

Genesis 2:18–24
Hebrews 2:9–11
Mark 10:2–16

Aim: To explore responsibility and faithfulness in caring for our world and in our relationships.

Starter

Play consequences. Each section is written and passed on around the circle, before the disjointed stories are read out. (Girl) met (boy) at (place). He said to her (…), she said to him (…), and the consequence was (…).

Teaching

Practically every book, film and T.V. show is about people and their relationships, falling in and out of love, marrying, divorcing, quarreling, making up and messing up. Today we are going to look at what the Bible teaches us about faithfulness and responsibility, both with one another and with the natural world.

Begin by reading the passage from Genesis, looking at the way humankind, in the person of Adam, is placed in a position of responsibility, to care for the world and look after it. Notice how lifelong partnership is seen as God's way of providing us with companionship and help, as we work under God's rule for the good of the world.

Now read today's gospel, where Jesus is teaching his disciples about divorce. He reminds them of the Genesis passage we have just read, reinforcing that God's way of faithfulness and responsibility in a lifelong relationship is good and rewarding. What does that mean for us as Christians, living in a time of easy divorce? It means we're going to need really serious thought and lots of prayer as we go about choosing a partner with whom we're expecting to spend the rest of our life, through the difficult times and broken nights, and financial worries and growing children, as well as the high spots and romantic bliss!

Praying

Lord, for ourselves;
in living power remake us—
self on the cross

and Christ upon the throne,
past put behind us,
for the future take us,
Lord of our lives,
to live for Christ alone.

(Taken from the song *Lord, for the years* by Timothy Dudley-Smith © 1969 Hope Publishing Co.)

Activities

On the activity sheet there is a questionnaire to help them look at choosing a marriage partner for life as a basis for discussion about this issue. Other callings in life are also explored. There is also space given to the responsible care of our universe, with examples of good and bad stewardship.

Discussion starters

1. Should our aim in life for ourselves and our children be happiness or goodness? How will this affect our attitude toward life's troubles and hardships?

2. What are the difficulties involved in taking Jesus' teaching on marriage seriously?

Notes

THE SINGLE LIFE

WHAT ABOUT OTHER CALLINGS ???

LIFE IN A COMMUNE

LIVING AS A MONK OR A NUN

UNITED NATIONS AIMS FOR AGREED POLICY ON FORESTATION

CUSTOMERS DEMAND FAIRLY TRADED COFFEE

FEWER AND FEWER PEOPLE TRAVEL BY PUBLIC TRANSPORT

INDUSTRIAL POLLUTION MADE BY VILLAGES IN INDIA

RESPONSIBILITY AND FAITHFULNESS

THAT SOUNDS LIKE HARD WORK.

True – but it's rewarding hard work. When we're being responsible and faithful in our relationships and in looking after our world, it feels 'right' for us.

WE CAN'T DO IT ALONE, THOUGH, CAN WE? No – it's a shared thing and is much easier if everyone joins in. But if others don't, that doesn't let us off.

DO YOU THINK GOD SOMETIMES GIVES US PARTICULAR JOBS OF RESPONSIBILITY TO DO? I'm certain of it. And when he does that, he also gives us the courage and strength to do them.

CHOOSING A MARRIAGE PARTNER

Number in order of importance

Someone you can be best friends with	
Someone who's rich	
Someone who shares your faith in God	
Someone you find physically attractive	
Someone you can be honest with	
Someone whose parents are nice	
Someone who does what you tell them	
Someone who shares your interests	
Someone who wants children	
Someone who respects you	

LORD, FOR OURSELVES;
IN LIVING POWER REMAKE US –
SELF ON THE CROSS
AND CHRIST UPON THE THRONE,
PAST PUT BEHIND US,
FOR THE FUTURE TAKE US:
LORD OF OUR LIVES,
TO LIVE FOR CHRIST ALONE.

(Taken from the song *Lord, For the Years* by
Timothy Dudley-Smith, © 1969 Hope Publishing Co.)

Twenty-eighth Sunday in Ordinary Time

Thought for the day

The most valuable possession is not the wealth that owns us, but is Christ, the Wisdom of God, who gives us untold riches.

Readings

Wisdom 7:7–11
Hebrews 4:12–13
Mark 10:17–30

Aim: To ask the young man's question.

Starter

Have two people turning a long jump rope. The others have to try getting through the rope without getting tangled.

Teaching

Have the words of the young man written down and explain that this was a question put to Jesus by a young man. Talk over what they would say to the young man if they were asked the question.

Now read today's gospel, with different people taking the various parts. How does Jesus' response compare with ours? Notice how he doesn't answer directly, but addresses what is going on in the man's mind as well as what he actually asks.

Next read the passage from Wisdom, looking at the importance of seeking God. God is found through the seeking. Go back to the gospel where the disciples ask how anyone at all can be saved, and see how Jesus tells them that this is impossible for us to do for ourselves; we need God for it, and then it becomes possible.

Finally read the passage from Hebrews, and think about what effect Jesus' words had on the young man, both immediately and possibly after he had calmed down a bit. The word of God is just as challenging to us, and just as effective, if we listen to it.

Praying

All that I dream, all that I pray,
all that I'll ever make I give to you today.
Take and sanctify these gifts
for your honor, Lord,
Knowing that I love and serve you
is enough reward.
All that I am, all that I do,
all that I'll ever have I offer now to you.

(Taken from the song *All That I Am* by Sebastian Temple
© 1967 OCP Publications, Portland, OR, USA)

Activities

The activity sheet reinforces the teaching in the gospel, with them taking a look at the things in their own lives that would be hard to give up, and a look at Christians who can witness to how they have gained through sacrificing things for Jesus.

Discussion starters

1. How can we help one another through the dark times when God does not seem to be answering us or making himself known?

2. What makes it so incredibly worthwhile to follow Jesus, in spite of the difficulties?

Notes

CONVENIENCE ITEMS

WASH 2000

POSSESSIONS

WHAT WOULD YOU FIND HARD TO GIVE UP IN ORDER TO FOLLOW JESUS?

DESIGNER CLOTHES

MONEY

POWER

ENTERTAINMENT

VIDEO

CAMEL THROUGH A NEEDLE

THAT'S IMPOSSIBLE! YOU'D NEVER GET A CAMEL THROUGH THE EYE OF A NEEDLE.

That's true. Why not?

WELL, THERE'S JUST TOO MUCH CAMEL!

Yes. Too much of riches works the same way.

DOES GOD EXPECT US ALL TO GIVE UP EVERYTHING?

We certainly need to live generously with others and simply with ourselves.

Mm. I'LL HAVE TO THINK ABOUT THAT.

HOW HARD IT IS FOR A RICH PERSON TO ENTER THE KINGDOM OF GOD!

IS IT WORTH GIVING UP RICHES FOR JESUS?

I kept telling myself I needed all my money and clothes purchases. I'd just buy for something to do. Finally I was brave enough to risk giving more away, and in a strange way I feel richer now than before! Wish I'd done it earlier.

I was a lawyer – lots of respect . . . high salary . . . and then I became a Christian and felt God calling me to give this life up to serve him in a particular (low paid!) way. And it's wonderful. Worth it many times over.

I trained as a youth worker and was offered a really well-paid job where I'd done my training. It seemed a good idea, but when I prayed about it I knew God was calling me to work with schools on Canvey Island. Money? I get expenses, that's all. But God looks after it. And it's brilliant to be doing God's work.

ALL THAT I DREAM, ALL THAT I PRAY
ALL THAT I'LL EVER MAKE
I GIVE TO YOU TODAY.
TAKE AND SANCTIFY THESE GIFTS
FOR YOUR HONOUR, LORD.
KNOWING THAT I LOVE AND SERVE YOU
IS ENOUGH REWARD.
ALL THAT I AM, ALL THAT I DO,
ALL THAT I'LL EVER HAVE
I OFFER NOW TO YOU.

(Taken from the song *All that I am*
by Sebastian Temple, © OCP Publications, USA)

I was on my way to spend some money on a couple of CDs and then go to a film. But I'd seen on the news all those people with no food. So I put the money aside for them instead. It was good to be able to help a little bit. And I still enjoyed myself.

Twenty-ninth Sunday in Ordinary Time

Thought for the day

Even the Son of Man himself came not to be served but to serve, and to give his life as a ransom for many.

Readings

Isaiah 53:10–11
Hebrews 4:14–16
Mark 10:35–45

Aim: To explore the concept of Jesus being a Servant King.

Starter

Human sculpture. One person is the sculptor, and the others are his medium to work with. He explains where he wants each person to be and how to arrange their body, until the whole group has turned into a sculpture. Then someone else can be the sculptor.

Teaching

Begin by reading the Isaiah passage. Here we see God's chosen One as a servant, suffering, humbled and broken, laying aside his majesty for the good of the world.

Go on to the reading from Hebrews, explaining that the Jewish priests were appointed to represent the people and offer sacrifices to God on their behalf. The writer points out that, owing to their own sinfulness, they needed to include themselves in this. Jesus, like a high priest, is also appointed by God, and becomes the perfect sacrifice to take away the sins of the whole world. (Link this with the Agnus Dei—"Lamb of God, you take away the sins of the world.")

Now read Mark 10:35–45, seeing how Jesus' calling to be the suffering servant ties in with the prophecies, and jars against what James and John are wanting. Like Jesus, we are called to the servant role.

Praying

My song is love unknown,
my Savior's love for me,
love to the loveless shown,
that they may lovely be.
O who am I, that for my sake,
my Lord should take frail flesh and die?

Activities

On the activity sheet they are helped to explore the concept of the suffering servant, which Jesus recog-nized as his route to save the world. There are also some examples of leadership to consider in the light of Jesus' teaching.

Discussion starters

1. Even if we grasp the idea of being servants, how can we stop ourselves striving to be the most important and highly honored servants of Christ?

2. Is Jesus' model for leadership practical? Do we practice it in the church and in our lives?

Notes

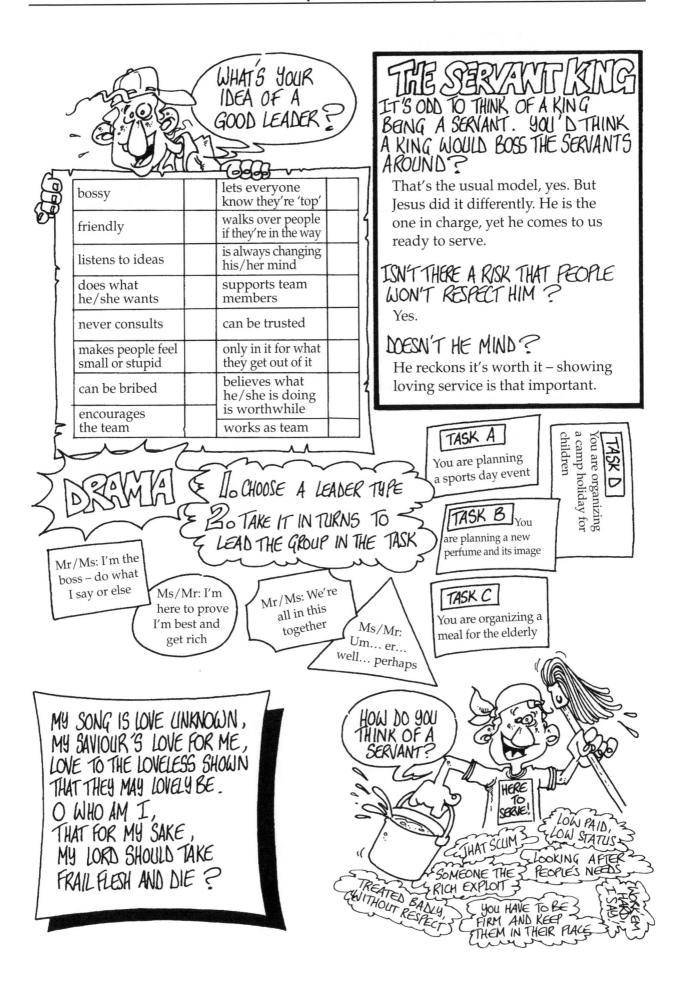

WHAT'S YOUR IDEA OF A GOOD LEADER?

bossy	lets everyone know they're 'top'	
friendly	walks over people if they're in the way	
listens to ideas	is always changing his/her mind	
does what he/she wants	supports team members	
never consults	can be trusted	
makes people feel small or stupid	only in it for what they get out of it	
can be bribed	believes what he/she is doing is worthwhile	
encourages the team	works as team	

THE SERVANT KING

IT'S ODD TO THINK OF A KING BEING A SERVANT. YOU'D THINK A KING WOULD BOSS THE SERVANTS AROUND?

That's the usual model, yes. But Jesus did it differently. He is the one in charge, yet he comes to us ready to serve.

ISN'T THERE A RISK THAT PEOPLE WON'T RESPECT HIM?

Yes.

DOESN'T HE MIND?

He reckons it's worth it – showing loving service is that important.

DRAMA

1. CHOOSE A LEADER TYPE
2. TAKE IT IN TURNS TO LEAD THE GROUP IN THE TASK

Mr/Ms: I'm the boss – do what I say or else

Ms/Mr: I'm here to prove I'm best and get rich

Mr/Ms: We're all in this together

Ms/Mr: Um… er… well… perhaps

TASK A
You are planning a sports day event

TASK B
You are planning a new perfume and its image

TASK C
You are organizing a meal for the elderly

TASK D
You are organizing a camp holiday for children

MY SONG IS LOVE UNKNOWN,
MY SAVIOUR'S LOVE FOR ME,
LOVE TO THE LOVELESS SHOWN
THAT THEY MAY LOVELY BE.
O WHO AM I,
THAT FOR MY SAKE,
MY LORD SHOULD TAKE
FRAIL FLESH AND DIE?

HOW DO YOU THINK OF A SERVANT?

HERE TO SERVE!

THAT SCUM

LOW PAID, LOW STATUS

LOOKING AFTER PEOPLE'S NEEDS

SOMEONE THE RICH EXPLOIT

TREATED BADLY, WITHOUT RESPECT

YOU HAVE TO BE FIRM AND KEEP THEM IN THEIR PLACE

Thirtieth Sunday in Ordinary Time

Thought for the day

In Jesus, God gathers his scattered people and opens their eyes to see.

Readings

Jeremiah 31:7–9
Hebrews 5:1–6
Mark 10:46–52

Aim: To see how, in Jesus, God gathers his scattered people back and opens their eyes to see.

Starter

Make a tape of assorted sounds. They have to figure out what the sounds are.

Teaching

With the aid of biblical maps, show how the split north kingdom of Israel was overcome by the Assyrians and the people taken into exile. Soon after that Assyria was attacked and conquered by the Babylonians.

Jeremiah lived in the south kingdom of Judah just after this, when Judah was caught in the middle between the Egyptians and the Babylonians. Before long Jerusalem itself would be captured and all except the poorest people of Judah deported to Babylon. Not happy times. Jeremiah was trying hard to warn the people that they really needed to unite under God's law, committing themselves to him completely.

Now read the passage from Jeremiah, with its picture of people returning to God with all their hearts. As we know, the people didn't listen, and they were taken into exile, eventually returning to a ruined city. But the hope developed that one day, a "son of king David" would be a special king, filled with God's power, who would lead his people back to God's ways.

Next look at the gospel, with different people reading the various parts. Here we have the blind man calling out to Jesus as "son of David." In Jesus that great hope has become a real person, walking around Jericho and the other cities, towns and villages, bringing people back to God and healing them. Today we have yet another example of such healing.

Praying

Praise, my soul, the King of heaven!
To his feet thy tribute bring;
ransomed, healed, restored, forgiven,
who like me his praise should sing?

Praise him! Praise him!
Praise him! Praise him!
Praise the everlasting King!

Activities

On the activity sheet there are examples of people returning after deportation, and they are encouraged to imagine the feelings at such a time. There are also examples of those who have returned to God after a long time of self-imposed exile, and how they feel. They can make a collage of returning with joy, using pictures, words and colors to express the sense of Psalm 126.

Discussion starters

1. In what way do Jesus' disciples help (or hinder) Bartimaeus from coming to Jesus for healing?

2. How do we help (or hinder) people from coming to Jesus?

Notes

Thirty-first Sunday in Ordinary Time

Thought for the day

To love the living God with heart, soul and strength, and to love our neighbor as ourselves means far more than any sacrificial offerings.

Readings

Deuteronomy 6:2–6
Hebrews 7:23–28
Mark 12:28–34

Aim: To see the priority of loving God.

Starter

Everyone makes their own favorite design paper plane, adjusting it for optimum flying. See whose can fly best and farthest.

Teaching

With the paper planes, the basic design was important, and also aligning and balancing, adjusting the shape to keep it from crashing. Today we are looking at getting our lives aligned and adjusted with the best design of all.

Read the passage from Deuteronomy, explaining that the people were just about to cross over into the Promised Land. What was their "design for living" going to be? How were they going to make sure it never got forgotten?

Tell them about the way the priests, on behalf of the people, regularly sacrificed animals, sprinkling the people with the animals' blood and offering the burnt sacrifice to God as a way of cleansing the people from sin. Show them some pictures of this. Now look at Hebrews 7:23–28, seeing how Jesus, being both the priest figure and the sacrificial victim (the Lamb of God), was able to do the cleansing of the people's sin once and for all. The people would understand about being "made clean" by the blood of animal sacrifices, so it made sense to them that the blood of Jesus, poured out for us on the cross, was able to cleanse us of sin completely.

Now explain how some of that offering of sacrifices had become empty ritual over the years, with the people doing all the actions, and having lots of rules about correct procedures, but living lives which were not in a loving relationship with God. The scribe in today's gospel was one of those who recognized this and worried about what really was important.

Read the gospel, so they can see how Jesus cut through all the accumulated complications, right to the very heart of the matter—loving the one true God with our whole heart and soul and mind and strength.

Praying

Be thou my vision, O Lord of my heart,
naught be all else to me save that thou art;
thou my best thought in the day and the night,
waking or sleeping, thy presence my light.

(From a song translated from the Irish
by Mary Byrne and Eleanor Hull © Copyright Control)

Activities

On the activity sheet there is a picture of the sacrifices being offered, together with the scribe's words in verse 33 of Mark 12. The children are encouraged to explore the difference between correct practices and a loving relationship. They also learn about the Shema, and the effect of Jesus reciting it in the context of his teaching.

Discussion starters

1. Jesus answers the seeking scribe's question not with argument but with a statement of faith. What can we learn from this?

2. What is our priority in life?

Notes

ANIMAL SACRIFICES OFFERED — TO TAKE AWAY THE PEOPLE'S SIN

CORRECT PRACTICE — OR THE REAL THING?

YOU MEAN LIKE GOING TO CHURCH EVERY WEEK BUT NOT REALLY TAKING GOD SERIOUSLY?

Yes, that's right. The Jewish people were going through all the ritual of sacrifices but they weren't always engaging with the real thing.

LOVING GOD, DO YOU MEAN?

Yes – that's having a real relationship with God, not being a robot.

WHY DID PEOPLE BOTHER WITH THE SACRIFICES IF THEY DIDN'T MEAN THEM?

They thought they'd do, instead of sorting their lives out.

NO WONDER IT ANNOYED JESUS!

THEN THE SACRIFICE WAS PLEASING TO GOD

YES

BUT DO THEIR LIVES SHOW THAT THEY ARE REALLY SORRY?

NO

THEN THEY MIGHT AS WELL NOT WASTE THEIR TIME AND MONEY DOING IT.

LOOK AT WHAT THE SCRIBE SAID TO JESUS: MARK 12:33

THE SHEMA

"Hear O Israel, the Lord our God is the one LorD"

THIS WAS THE GREAT STATEMENT OF FAITH FOR EVERY JEWISH PERSON.

WHAT DO YOU NOTICE ABOUT THE FIRST AND LAST LETTERS?

THAT'S BECAUSE IN HEBREW THEY MADE THE WORD 'WITNESS'

BE THOU MY VISION, O LORD OF MY HEART, NAUGHT BE ALL ELSE TO ME SAVE THAT THOU ART; THOU MY BEST THOUGHT IN THE DAY AND THE NIGHT, WAKING OR SLEEPING, THY PRESENCE MY LIGHT.

(From a song translated from the Irish by Mary Byrne and Eleanor Hull © Copyright Control)

IMAGINE THE IMPACT OF JESUS, THE SON OF GOD, RECITING THE SHEMA!

Thirty-second Sunday in Ordinary Time

Thought for the day
Loving generosity is the hallmark of Godly giving.

Readings
1 Kings 17:10–16
Hebrews 9:24–28
Mark 12:38–44

Aim: To look at God's view of generosity.

Starter
Bring along something everyone enjoys eating, and say that as you were feeling generous today you thought you'd like to treat everyone. Share out the food to be eaten later, and enjoy the sudden burst of generosity!

Teaching
In our readings today we are going to be looking at God's view of generosity, and we're starting with a story of a generous-hearted widow in the Old Testament. Read the passage from 1 Kings 17, with different voices reading the parts of Elijah and the woman. The woman's remarkable generosity to Elijah was returned to her by a blessing for her and her son.

Now look at today's gospel, with another widow story. (Widows were very often poor and destitute.) Why was this woman commended for her generosity when she'd given such a little? Discuss what connection generosity has to amount and attitude, drawing out the way God is most concerned about the loving, wholeheartedness of our giving.

Finally look at the amazing example in Hebrews of loving generosity shown in Christ offering nothing less than himself. How can we respond to this amount of generous love?

Praying
Were the whole realm of nature mine,
that were an offering far too small;
love so amazing, so divine,
demands my soul, my life, my all.

Activities
On the activity sheet the story of Elijah and the widow encourages them to go behind the spoken words to the possible thought processes. They also look at how seeming generosity can actually be pride, ambition or boasting, and explore what qualities mark genuine generosity.

Discussion starters
1. Is it practical to live in the world without being taken over by worldly values?
2. Are there any ways we can take more seriously the call to practice hospitality?

Notes

Thirty-third Sunday in Ordinary Time

Thought for the day

We are to be on our guard; great anguish will accompany the last days, but all that is good and loving, wise and true will be saved and celebrated forever.

Readings

Daniel 12:1–3
Hebrews 10:11–14, 18
Mark 13:24–32

Aim: To explore how the kingdom of heaven is both in the present and the future.

Starter

Beforehand make a number of inkblot shapes on different pieces of paper, and invite everyone to say what pictures they see in the inkblots.

Teaching

In inkblots, clouds and shadows, we can often see pictures. Some people would say that what we see shows our character! Today's readings look into the misty future—to the end of time, and two prophets tell us what they see. One of the prophets is Daniel, and the other is Jesus himself.

First read the passage from Daniel. What pictures does the prophet see? Is it terrifying, hopeful, or a mixture? On a sheet of paper headed "At that time," write the events in different colored pens to reflect their mood.

Now look at the gospel for today. Once again, write the events on the sheet in different colored pens. Does Jesus seem to be excited about this time, or concerned for his followers? What is it that bothers him? He is wanting to impress on his followers the need to be careful and on our guard, in readiness for these times.

We are left with the sense that it will be a frightening time leading up to the Day of the Lord, with evil multiplying and many being led astray. But there is still the strong certainty that through it all the true followers will be kept safe, and nothing good or loving will be lost. Whatever people are really like will be shown for everyone to see—our motives and secret thoughts, as well as what we choose to let people see normally. It's quite a thought.

Praying

You show me the path of life;
in your presence there is fullness of joy,
and in your right hand are pleasures for evermore.

(From Psalm 16)

Activities

On the activity sheet they are encouraged to see how the kingdom of heaven is both now and in the future, and there is space for them to try a water-color painting of the Daniel or the Mark reading.

Discussion starters

1. Are we worried about the right things, or about things which needn't concern us?

2. Do today's readings affect our attitude toward evangelization?

Notes

A WATERCOLOUR PAINTING, BASED ON DANIEL 12: 1-3 OR MARK 13: 24-32

THE DAY OF THE LORD

WILL THERE BE AN ACTUAL, REAL DAY WHEN EVERYTHING AS WE KNOW IT COMES TO AN END?

Yes, we are told by the prophets and by Jesus himself. We don't know when or how, but we do know it will happen.

IS THAT WHEN THE KINGDOM OF GOD WILL COME?

Yes and no! Yes, it will come totally when we see Jesus coming in glory as judge and gatherer. But we don't have to wait till then – the kingdom is already here wherever God's will is done and wherever Jesus is allowed to reign.

IN MY LIFE, FOR INSTANCE?

Exactly!

SIGNS OF THE KINGDOM NOW

SIGNS OF THE DAY OF THE LORD TO LOOK FOR

YOU SHOW ME THE PATH OF LIFE; IN YOUR PRESENCE THERE IS FULLNESS OF JOY, AND IN YOUR RIGHT HAND ARE PLEASURES FOR EVERMORE.

(– FROM PSALM 15 –)

Christ the King

Thought for the day

Jesus Christ is the everlasting King whose kingdom is not of this world, but grows in the hearts of his people and lasts forever.

Readings

Daniel 7:13–14
Revelation 1:5–8
John 18:33–37

Aim: To recognize Jesus Christ as the everlasting King of all.

Starter

Give everyone a large post-it note on which they write ten sentences beginning with "I am…" Then they stick their note to themselves and go around reading one another's statements.

Teaching

It's not easy to decide on ten "I am…" statements, but taken altogether they do give a little idea of who we are. Today, the last Sunday of the church's year, we are in a way summing up everything we know about Jesus Christ, both on earth and in heaven, and the shorthand for all of that is that he is Christ the King. We'll try to understand it a bit.

Begin by reading Daniel's vision. Point out that Daniel was writing long before Jesus had come, yet he "sees" Jesus entering heaven and being made king.

Now go to the gospel, reading it with different people taking the different parts. Pilate's job, as Roman governor, is to establish whether this so-called king is likely to pose a threat to the Roman empire. As Jesus says, that would be so if his kingdom were "of this world." But it isn't. In what way is the kingdom of heaven not "of this world"? If the territory of the kingdom of heaven is not geographical, where is it found? (Think back to the parables of the kingdom, and all Jesus' teaching about kingdom living.)

So today we see Jesus at his most weak and vulnerable, humanly speaking, on earth, and entering heaven in glory. All of that is the same Jesus, the Servant King who was obedient even to death on a cross.

Finally look at the reading from Revelation, where Jesus Christ is seen as the faithful witness, the firstborn from the dead, and the ruler of the kings of the earth. We are reminded that Jesus is the visible image of the unseen God, totally faithful to speaking out God's words and revealing his love to us. And one day he will come in glory, seen by everybody.

As we look back over the past year, and all we have learned of Jesus, it makes us want to worship and proclaim with Christians all over the world and all through history that Jesus Christ is Lord!

Praying

Jesus is Lord!
Creation's voice proclaims it,
for by his power each tree and flower
was planned and made.
Jesus is Lord!
The universe declares it;
sun, moon and stars in heaven cry:
Jesus is Lord!

(Taken from the song *Jesus is Lord!* by David J. Mansell © 1982 Word's Spirit of Praise/Maranatha! Music/Copyright Co.)

Activities

In the activities on the sheet they are helped to hold in balance the power and glory of Jesus' kingship with his humility and obedience—the Servant King. They try to catch hold of the image of heaven as described by Daniel, and look at the idea of the words of the Gloria and God's presence in past, present and future.

Discussion starters

1. How does this faith we celebrate today transform our outlook and enable us to face suffering?

2. What is your vision of heaven?

Notes

NOT OF THIS WORLD

BUT JESUS CAME INTO THIS WORLD, DIDN'T HE? HOW COME HIS KINGDOM IS NOT OF THIS WORLD THEN?

When John writes about 'the world' he isn't thinking of God's wonderful good creation. He means 'worldly', or looking for selfish pleasure and greed.

SO JESUS ISN'T SAYING THE WORLD IS OUTSIDE HIS KINGDOM?

Oh no – God's natural world is part of the kingdom. But Jesus is not a king of a country, like wanting to be another Julius Caesar or something.

WHERE IS HE KING, THEN?

Wherever people love God and love one another. Wherever they invite Jesus to reign.

DRAW IN THE RIGHT BALANCE FOR YOUR CURRENT FAVOURITE CD—

BALANCE ─ ▯ ▯ ▯ ▯ ─ D
— GRAPHIC EQUALIZER —
VOLUME 0 1 2 3 4 5 6 7 8 9 10 11 12

WE HAVE TO GET THE BALANCE RIGHT...

JESUS IS BOTH KING OF GLORY AND POWER ...

... AND THE ONE WHO HUMBLY SERVES OTHERS

WHO WAS

AND IS

AND WILL BE

DANIEL 7: 13-14

JESUS IS LORD!
CREATION'S VOICE PROCLAIMS IT,
FOR BY HIS POWER
EACH TREE AND FLOWER
WAS PLANNED AND MADE.
JESUS IS LORD!
THE UNIVERSE DECLARES IT;
SUN, MOON AND STARS
IN HEAVEN CRY:
JESUS IS LORD!

(Taken from the song *Jesus is Lord!*
by David J. Mansell, © 1982 World's Spirit of
Praise/Maranatha! Music/Copyright Co.)

Appendix

Mark What's up?

Dawn Uh? Oh, nothing.

Mark But there's a Fuse bar here that you haven't eaten.

Dawn Uh? Oh, so there is.

Mark And I haven't had any e-mail from you for over a week.

Dawn Uh? Oh . . . no, I haven't written any.

Mark Well, what's the matter for heaven's sake?

Dawn *(sighs)* Well, it's no use.

Mark What's no use?

Dawn Everything's no use. Only one person has the key to my freedom and peace of mind, and I'm trapped in this prison.

Mark Well, ask the person with the key to open it!

Dawn That's just it – I can't.

Mark Why ever not?

Dawn Because I've completely ignored the person with the key for ages, and before that I messed up their life big time. So there's no reason in the world why they should even be friendly ever again – let alone get me out of my mess now.

Mark You could ask them.

Dawn No, it's too late for that. I'll just have to recognize that I've blown it for ever.

Mark Well, you could still ask. Maybe he's super-human in the mercy line. Maybe he still cares for you enough to come and rescue you.

Dawn Do you think so?

Mark No harm in trying, is there? After all, he did create you.

Dawn Yes, that's true. OK. Let's ask him.

Both O Lord God, I know you've got no reason to hear this prayer after the way we've treated you, but, well, you did make us, remember? Could you find it in your heart to come and rescue us? Sort us out? We need that so badly, and we can't do it ourselves . . .

(A paper dart comes flying in, and they read what is written on it)

Both 'For God so loved the world that he gave his one and only Son, that whoever believes in him shall not perish but have eternal life.'

(They look at one another in excitement, and throw the paper dart up into the air as both shout: YES!)

The Servant

The employer is talking on his mobile phone, pacing up and down, with a file open. He's sorting out some complex problem. The office cleaner comes in with feather duster and starts cleaning.

Mr. King (Into phone) Quite . . . Quite . . . But look at these figures on page 24 . . . *(catches sight of Marg the cleaner)* Marg, get me a strong coffee. And a doughnut or something. *(Returns to phone)* Yes, these figures should have warned us . . . Well, the point is what can we do about it now?

(Marg reappears with coffee and doughnut.)

Marg Coffee, Mr. King. It's strong. And a doughnut. *(Puts them on desk)*

Mr. King *(Still on phone, listening and making 'mm' noises. Motions with hand for Marg not to interrupt him as he's busy.)* Sorry, Steve, say that again . . . the schedules systematically reduced what? . . . Oh, I see. Yes, of course. So what are you going to do about it?

(Marg continues dusting.)

Mr. King *(Still on phone)* Marg, get me the February file—it's there on my desk. *(Talks into phone)* It seems to me we can possibly get ourselves out of this mess, Steve. I've just had an idea.

(Marg brings the February file to Mr. King.)

Marg The February file, Mr. King.

Mr. King *(Takes it without thanking her and starts looking in it. Into phone he says)* Yes, here it is! I'm looking at these figures for the second week of February . . .

(Marg goes back to the dusting. The desk phone rings.)

Mr. King Answer that, Marg.

Marg *(Picks up phone)* Hello, Mr. King's office. Well, he's very busy at the moment, in an important meeting . . . Oh, I've no idea, I'm only the cleaner here. I just do what I'm told.

The Friends

Norman and Pete walk up to a bench and sit down. They put their rucksacks down.

Pete Phew! That was quite a climb, wasn't it. What a view, though, eh?

Norman Marvellous, isn't it. *(Pause)* Anyway, you were saying about your interview . . .

Pete Oh yeah, that's right. So we've got to decide whether to move or not, basically. And that's a big decision to make.

Norman How does Sheila feel about moving? She settled here, isn't she?

Pete Yes, it would be quite a wrench for her, but you know Sheila, she's willing to give it a go if she feels it's what God wants for us.

Norman Funny, isn't it. This time last year, there you were just made redundant, and no hopes for the future, and now this new door seems to be opening for you. I'm really happy for you, Pete.

Pete Thanks, Norman. Well, you've been a good friend through all this—it's always good to talk things over with you. Shall we be on our way then? *(They get up and walk off.)*

All four characters I no longer call you servants, because a servant doesn't know his master's business. Instead I have called you friends.

Cast your cares
on the Lord.
(Psalm 55:22)

Come unto me all who
labor and are heavy
laden, and I will give
you rest.
(Matthew 11:28)

He will direct your paths.
(Proverbs 3:6)

Small is the gate and
narrow the road that
leads to life.
(Matthew 7:13)

He will not suffer your
foot to be moved.
(Psalm 121:3)

He owns the cattle on a
thousand hills.
(Psalm 50:10)

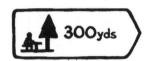

I am the bread of life.
(John 6:35)

Be self-controlled
and alert.
(1 Peter 5:8)

Life's an uphill struggle
without Jesus.